Dr. Lee Ann B. Marino, Ph.D., D.Min., D.D.

THE FUNDAMENTALS

OF

CHRISTIAN COUNSELING

IN THEORY AND PRACTICE

THE FUNDAMENTALS OF CHRISTIAN COUNSELING

IN THEORY AND PRACTICE
(First Edition)

Dr. Lee Ann B. Marino, Ph.D., D.Min., D.D.

Published by:
Righteous Pen Publications
(An imprint of the Righteous Pen Publications Group)
www.righteouspenpublications.com

Book Classification: Religion & Spirituality > Religious Studies > Counseling

ISBN: 1940197082
13-Digit: 978-1-940197-08-1

Printed in the United States of America.

For who among men knows the *thoughts* of a man except the spirit of the man which is in him? Even so the *thoughts* of God no one knows except the Spirit of God. Now we have received, not the spirit of the world, but the Spirit who is from God, so that we may know the things freely given to us by God, which things we also speak, not in words taught by human wisdom, but in those taught by the Spirit, combining spiritual *thoughts* with spiritual *words.*

But a natural man does not accept the things of the Spirit of God, for they are foolishness to him; and he cannot understand them, because they are spiritually appraised. But he who is spiritual appraises all things, yet he himself is appraised by no one. For who has known the mind of the Lord, that he will instruct Him? But we have the mind of Christ.

- 1 Corinthians 2:10-16

TABLE OF CONTENTS

INTRODUCTION

What is Counseling?

Where no counsel is, the people fall: but in the multitude of counsellors there is safety.
- Proverbs 11:14 (KJV)

*M*erriam-Webster's Online Dictionary defines "counseling" as "Professional guidance of the individual by utilizing psychological methods especially in collecting case history data, using various techniques of the personal interview, and testing interests and aptitudes."[1] This formalized textbook definition merely scratches the surface of the depth of counseling and its purpose, speaking more on method or procedure. It is obvious according to this definition, therefore, that if people define counseling just like this, counseling is missing essential divine components that can change and transform the lives of those receiving counseling.

Counseling is far more than procedure and protocol. It is not hit and miss, nor is it something by which we try different things until we find one that works. Counseling is the application of divine wisdom to specific instances and circumstances. While the means by which this divine wisdom may come about does vary, the application of counseling to life circumstances exists to bring about God's revelation.

Events, meetings, and other public ministry works are awesome examples of a dispensation of revelation given to a group of people at one time. God can move in a powerful way, especially in the lives of His individual people present. The way God moves in a public arena shows up and shows out that God is real and alive and active in the work of His saints and in the lives of His people. It's great and powerful work but is not always the way wisdom is dispensed in the life of an individual.

Counseling is a means by which God reveals directly to an individual by His private revelation. It reaches out to the individual wherever they are and relates directly to an individual's specific situation and issue at hand. It raises specific healing for hurts and areas in need of guidance, and watches God's loving hand reach out and take the person exactly where they need to go.

Counseling is also unique in that it is a revelation the person receives within themselves. Modern-day styles of preaching and teaching have introduced the principle of "drive-by" revelation into the church: the preacher brings the message that reflects what God is speaking to them, about them, or for them, and they, in turn, present that revelation unto their audiences. Whether the audience receives it or not, but it is not tailored to meet a specific need or interest in each individual person. There is a place for "drive-by" revelation, and it is in the pulpit and public preaching or teaching ministry. I use the term "drive-by" not to be pejorative, but to illustrate the concept: everyone present receives the same thing and it hits or misses people. Counseling is different in that it is not hit-or-miss: it is exacting. It reaches the person right where they are, and the revelation comes forth from them.

The Bible tells us that there is "wisdom in counsel" (Proverbs 11:14). Even though counseling is not as exalted as public ministry, it is just as relevant. In counseling it is more relevant how the minister interacts with the individual, treats the individual, and handles the situation with confidentiality and integrity. It also means that the minister of God must be trained for every good work, purposed and prepared to assist the work of ministry through counseling.

The anointing required for counseling

Counseling falls under the heading of a prophetic gift. While it does, in some ways, relate to the pastoral as well (because it is a work of guidance), one does not need to be a pastor to function in it, because the prophetic gifts one has will suffice. To serve as a counselor effectively and powerfully, a person must walk in the prophetic in some way in their anointing. As a prophetic gift, God can give it to anyone (prophecy and prophetic gifts belong to the body of believers, with its administration overseen by the office of the prophet), and the regulation of its operation moves through the apostles and prophets. In its execution, the following other spiritual gifts relate to counseling:

- **Prophecy:** The broad category of prophecy is often divided down into many different divisions or facets based upon the gifts one may have that relate to prophecy. By prophecy an individual conveys God's message to His people. Prophecy is the ability to reveal the purposes of God, the heart of God, walk in unspoken divine knowledge, and bring forth the resulting consequences of a word, action, or event. This can be done futuristically (as in prophesying a specific consequence for an action – the exile into Babylon, for example), specifically futuristic (the prophesy of the Messiah's birth), or specific to a circumstance, action, or behavior (knowing the consequence of a doing by the Spirit). Prophecy can work in dreams, in creativity, in words spoken or uttered, teaching, encouragement, guidance, and yes, especially through counseling. By the prophetic, a counselor can know what is needed and the necessary moral, practical, and spiritual guidance that must be transferred through counseling.

- **Prayer:** Prayer is an essential component of Christian counseling because prayer is our communication with God. Counselors should pray for divine guidance and wisdom. Through prayer, counselors learn about effective communication and the essential keys to hearing from God as well as relaying God's message.

- **Intercession:** Intercession is not simply a form of prayer, as we, in church, are commonly taught. Intercession is the literal wrangling between heaven and earth by which an individual petitions and, for lack of a better term, wrestles with God as they view things from a human perspective. As God reveals the heavenly position, they see both sides, and continue to wrangle, now both for the human and the divine. It is the literal veil, the meeting place of heaven and earth in the life and movement of the prophetic. It is more than just praying for other people, as the intercessor literally takes the issue on themselves: petitioning, struggling, and hope for the desired outcome. It's not merely a style of prayer. It's an entire way of viewing the divine, the prophetic, what is human, and what is divine, as one gains a glimpse into both that which is eternal and temporal for the hope of humanity's redemption.

- **Word of Knowledge:** To give a word of knowledge is to give a word providing information about something that comes from divine revelation. It may pertain to a person's situation or something about that individual. The specific intent in a word of knowledge is to let someone know God is with them, for them, and aware of things in their lives. It may also provide knowledge or insight into someone's situation, thus requiring the obedience of the individual to bring the matter to pass.

- **Word of Wisdom:** A word of wisdom is just what it sounds like: it is the delivery of wisdom applicable to a specific situation. When one gives a word of wisdom, they are delivering God's wisdom to an individual or to a group of people. Word of wisdom relates to an individual's obedience in that they must apply the necessary wisdom to action to see God's hand and wisdom work in their lives.

- **Discernment:** Never underestimate the role of spirits and spiritual activity when it comes to matters of counseling. A discerning spirit goes a very long way in counseling. Counselors need to know when they are being lied to, when spirits are at work in people's lives, and what is going on spiritually that may not be seen. Discernment helps fill in the gaps, read people better, and assist in the necessary discovery of a solution.

- **Faith:** A good counselor knows that with God, all things are possible. We also know that God does not do things in people's lives against their will. If someone doesn't want to be healed or helped, they won't be. But for those who do want to be helped, we know the power of faith in healing. God can and will reach out to those who are sincere by the power of faith and trust in Him and bring about a lasting change that only God can bring about.

We will look later in this text at the different ways different offices of the five-fold operate in counseling. The gifts listed above help an individual be an effective counselor, whether one predominately operates one of the above-mentioned gifts or several of them. The combination of God's gifts bring each of God's counselors to a place where they can impact and change lives for the greater glory of God.

Types of counseling

There are three main "types" of counseling: therapy, counseling, and counsel.

- **Therapy** is counseling used as a therapeutic tool to correct a mental illness, psychological issue, or behavioral problem. The application for therapy is done through a series of counseling sessions by which a certain school of therapeutic practice (something done repeatedly to gain a desired result) or a combination of different practices are put into action. Therapy often includes the use of medication, group workshops or practices, and is very therapist-specific and centered. The results of therapy are mixed and studies for therapy are often inconclusive. What seems to work for some does not work for all. The goal of therapy is to treat a problem or disorder, helping the individual to maintain as normal a state of being as possible.

- **Counseling** is the application of some therapeutic practice, some behavior modification, and other assorted tools (many interactive) to help people solve specific issues or problems. Unlike therapy, medication is not a part of the work of a counselor. Counseling is more advice-based, while still encouraging the client to receive the necessary insight to solve the problems they may have. It is often interactive, encouraging behavior modification, insight, and introspection into circumstances through a variety of means. The counselor equips the seeking individual with the necessary tools, approach, and thought processes to handle life, problems, and find answers in life.

- **Counsel** is a process by which someone gives another person advice. The advice either pertains to a specific situation or pertains across the board to life direction or life meaning in general. The most philosophical of the three, counseling gives direct advice rather than attempting to work so the individual discovers tools and approaches to help with issues and life in general.

Areas of counseling

There are numerous different areas of counseling in existence today. Counseling, as a profession, has become very popular in the past few years, especially as people major in one area of study (psychology or social work, for example) and then specialize in an area of counseling that interests them.

There are six major areas of "counseling" and some of their subheadings below:

- **Psychiatry**: Psychiatry is the study of mental disorders. Psychiatric counseling falls under the heading of therapy. Psychiatrists vary from psychologists and other counselors in that they do have medical degrees and are legally allowed to prescribe medications to their patients. The work of psychiatry is a more extensive counseling than that used by other counselors, and often includes intensive medical specializations and work with a broader audience. Psychiatrists are extensively trained, familiar with differing areas of mental health, and duly prepared to assist those they work with. It is worth noting, however, that psychiatrists often specialize in certain areas of psychiatric practice or psychological study (such as Jung, Freud, etc.), and in certain areas of therapy (marriage and family, mental health, etc.).

- **Psychology**: Psychology is the study of the mind, especially as how it relates to human behavior. Psychological counseling can fall under the heading of either therapy (minus the use of medicine) or counseling as a technique and approach. Most often psychology focuses more on counseling and specifically working a process with people than trying to treat disorders. Psychological counseling also relates to the way that the mind works and how human behavior can be changed or modified.

- **Medical**: Counseling is also used in the medical field to modify, educate, or treat certain medical issues. It can also be used to help patients with difficult diagnoses (such as cancer or HIV). Counseling to improve or change diet, nutrition, or to aid in the treatment of substance abuse are common. Doctors, nurses, registered dieticians or specifically trained individuals in different areas of medicine may all work in counseling, depending on their specialty, field, or treatment position (hospital, facility, etc.)

- **Legal**: A lawyer has historically been called a "counselor" because a lawyer acts upon the law and dispenses legal advice. A lawyer may still give legal advice today, but their function is more as legal counsel than as a counselor.

- **Education**: The traditional role of the Guidance Counselor in a school was to help a student select a career. In modern times the role of Guidance Counselor extends to helping students with difficult situations at home, at school, or emotional or mental problems that can inhibit learning. The role of a Guidance

Counselor is different from a school psychiatrist or psychologist, although the two may work together.

- **Social work**: Social work is a broad category of counseling that relates to issues affecting human beings. Social workers deal with issues that affect people, such as divorce, poverty, adoption, unemployment, welfare, immigration, prison, social injustices, and other issues that are like these. The goal of one involved with social work is to improve the life and conditions of life for people or a group of people. Although a social worker is not necessarily always one who may do counseling in social work, a degree in social work or psychology is required at minimum to operate a paid and licensed counseling facility that is not religious or charitable in nature.

- **Special interest counseling**: Special interest counseling relates to areas of social interest that are limited to or relate to a specific area in scope. Each area of special interest counseling has its own unique set of criteria and may or may not have recognized affiliations or licenses by which to associate oneself with. Examples of special interest counseling include debt relief, life coaching, job coaching, and certified professional organizers.

- **Spiritual/religious**: Spiritual or religious-based counseling is different from other forms of counseling in one major way: it incorporates the divine (whatever the concept the counselor or those receiving counseling may have of the divine) into the counseling technique. The basis for counseling is, therefore, spiritual or religious, centering the individual in spiritual precepts rather than in a specific school of thought or approach to problem solving. Spiritual or religious counseling often draws on common secular counseling techniques while incorporating belief into the mix to help overcome various tendencies or aid in behavior modification. Spiritual and religious counseling is largely unregulated, but within the United States, ministers practicing counseling must have a valid minister's license and ordination to be deemed legitimate. Because religious counseling is largely unregulated under the heading of religious belief and practice, any number of unorthodox or dangerous counseling techniques may be employed by unsupervised individuals. Some may engage in exorcisms where people are beaten or whipped, attendees may be subject to hours of preaching on end, or a deceptive leader may try to engage vulnerable, seeking people into more dangerous physical or spiritual abuses. As this book focuses on Christian counseling, it is essential that we maintain ethics and obedience to God in our practices as good representatives of all Christian counseling can offer.

Purposes for counseling

There isn't one specified set of reasons someone may require counseling. The need for counseling may be long-term or short-term. Because the purpose of counseling is to receive specific divine revelation, there are any number of reasons why someone may seek out counseling. Some specific reasons include:

- Seeking out guidance as pertains to a calling or anointing on one's life
- Marital or family issues
- Depression
- Divorce
- Death of a loved one or friend
- Needed change in life
- Fears or anxieties
- Realization of abuse or trauma
- Desire to change behaviors
- Struggles with addiction or compulsive behaviors
- Needing to hear from God
- Seeking a deeper walk or relationship with God

One of the biggest assumptions that people make about counseling is that people only seek out counseling when something bad happens or when they have a severe, serious problem in their lives. This is not necessarily the case. Counseling is needed as people seek specific and direct revelation from God. Not every reason someone seeks out counseling is negative or related to a traumatic event. The above-mentioned list is provided to show that there are many different reasons someone may need or seek out counseling that have nothing to do with anything negative.

It is also a mistake to assume that because someone needs counseling that they are not getting what they need in their general relationship with God or experience in church. Sometimes it is true they are not getting what they need spiritually, and a good counselor operating in discernment will discern this through the counseling process. In that situation, it is essential to make sure that the needs are addressed and met as part of the hands-on process. Sometimes the issue at hand, however, has nothing to do with any of that – sometimes it is just a circumstance where revelation needs to be revealed through counseling.

Good counselors ask what the matter or pressing issue at hand is and seek God's guidance as to the next stages and phases of development. They do not guess on matters or put their clients on the offensive. After meeting the client, the process of counseling begins and both technique and spiritual gifts combine to help the patient wherever they may be in their lives.

When is counseling needed?

Counseling can be needed at any point in one's life. In a Christian setting, counseling is needed whenever group ministering and individual devotion are not enough to help someone beyond a point, challenge or circumstance. There is no shame in needing divine guidance through counseling.

The need for counseling often signalizes a "passages phase" of spiritual development. A passages phase symbolizes the transition from one issue or level to another, and the internal conflict which results during that passage. A major change may have occurred, but that is not always the case. When counseling is needed, people know a change is needed. It can be a big change or a small change, but the resulting change comes about because God is somehow speaking to an individual about their circumstances. In that state of change, people seek out guidance through counseling.

Counseling is also needed on a regular basis when someone is struggling with a problem that controls one's life or many aspects of one's life. The mentally ill need to be under the constant supervision of a qualified and trained professional for the monitor of conditions that may trigger emotional or mental cycling. People battling long-term issues (such as depression or realization of abuse) may also need the help obtained through counseling.

Goals of counseling

Depending on the circumstances at hand, the goals of counseling vary between patients, at least on the surface. A mentally ill patient may have the goal of maintaining as normal a life as possible through counseling. Someone working to overcome abuse may seek healing. The underlying goal of every counseling session is to solve the issues at hand and walk toward finding a better life.

What is special about Christian counseling?

Christian counseling is special because it is Christ-centered. Other counseling programs may bring forth some benefit and help people in their lives to a certain extent, but they miss the essential component of Christ-centered identity. If we are to be successful in life, victorious over problems, and maintain peace, balance, and order in our lives, we need to know who we are in Christ.

True Christian counseling roots an individual in success in the following ways:

- **Knowing who they are in Christ:** If we don't know who we are in Christ, we do not know who we are as we stand before God. To be healthy, productive members of both God's Kingdom and society, we need to know who we are in Christ: that we are sanctified, saved, loved, and forgiven. We need to understand ourselves as men and women of God's Kingdom before we understand ourselves as anything else.

- **Knowing their purpose in Christ:** Only when we are in Christ do we come to know our true purpose. This gives us a sense of stability and order as we pursue a true purpose rather than a false one. Our purpose in Christ is whatever God has given for us to do. It is not just being called to ministry, but whatever someone's call is to life.

- **Having a sense of vision in Christ:** Knowing the Lord and understanding His purpose in one's life as Lord and Savior gives people a new outlook on life. New perspective, new hope, new promises for healing, and a clean slate remind us that despite faults, failings, and problems of the past, we can continue because of His work within us.

- **Understand the principles of the Spirit and how the Spirit helps us with issues in our lives:** Unlike most conventional methods of psychiatric therapy or psychological approach, the Word of God helps us to understand that we do have the power to change our behavior and change our circumstances. Contrary to what may be regarded as popular belief, we are not merely subject to uncontrollable impulses. We can walk in self-control. We can walk in forgiveness. We can operate in a spirit of love. We can find our direction from God's Word and follow God's precepts unto life. We can find order in disorder. Knowing this is more empowering and purposed than believing one's life is controlled by impulse or random fate.

Chapter Review

Construct a well-written essay (minimum 5-8 sentences each), answering the following question.

- Describe the six areas of counseling and how those six areas of counseling help individuals to address various issues they may have in their lives.

SECTION I

A Brief History of Counseling in Theory and Practice

CHAPTER ONE

The Relevance in the Foundations of Modern Counseling

Please inquire of past generations, And consider the things searched out by their fathers.
For we are only of yesterday and know nothing, Because our days on earth are as a shadow.
Will they not teach you and tell you, And bring forth words from their minds?
- Job 8:8-10

The history and evolution of counseling is a fascinating look at the way society has sought to deal with its problems. The analysis, introspection, and different theories reflect thoughts of the times past and thoughts of our times, as well.

Christian counseling tends to ignore the history of counseling practice and attempts to create its own concepts of counseling. What many fail to realize is most Christian counseling techniques are adaptations of secular counseling methods. If we reject the full history of counseling, we also reject our own role as Christian counselors. Those who pioneered various fields of counseling and psychological study were from diverse backgrounds, philosophical understandings, and approaches to heal the human psyche. Each area of study offers us something to use, think about, and consider as we approach the whole of Christian counseling and the integration of well-being in the whole person. We need to consider different approaches, techniques, and thoughts to balance the whole of our practice as we approach counseling from a whole perspective.

As Christian counselors, we must be duly prepared to handle any number of problems, issues, and complications that may arise with our patients. The way we prepare ourselves is by understanding different forms of theory and technique. People are complicated and often bring with them complicated issues. Seeing the different ways a patient can be approached gives us an important edge in preparation and the ability to empower ourselves and our patients as we approach their healing and patient care.

Counseling has transcended over time. In its original founding, counseling served to assist and study the mentally ill. Nowadays people seek out counseling for any number of reasons, spanning from marriage preparation to overcoming childhood problems. Once upon a time, counseling was reserved for those with severe mental disturbances or neurosis. Watching counseling evolve from an application for the very troubled to a general consultation for life is a fascinating process. With these shifts have come differences in approach, theory, and practice.

Even though we may not agree with every aspect of counseling theories and practices, it is important we review them to understand the different techniques applied in counseling today. In this chapter we will look at the major counseling theories and practices spanning the modern history of counseling: Sigmund Freud, Carl Jung, Alfred Adler, Abraham Maslow, B.F. Skinner, Karen Horney, Melanie Klein, and Erich Fromm.

SIGMUND FREUD

CHAPTER TWO

Sigmund Freud, Father of Modern Psychotherapy

But I see a different law in the members of my body,
waging war against the law of my mind
and making me a prisoner of the law of sin which is in my members.
- Romans 7:23

igmund Freud, born Sigismund Schlomo Freud (1856-1939), is considered the father of modern psychotherapy. He was an Austrian Jew who, although not associating himself with the religious practices of Judaism, considered himself a Jew throughout the whole of his life. He was a neurologist whose work led to the development of psychoanalysis (a term he coined himself), the foundational technique used in all modern counseling. The tenets of psychoanalysis are, as follows[1]:

- Human behavior, experience, and cognition are largely determined by irrational drives;
- Those drives are largely unconscious;
- Attempts to bring those drives into awareness meet psychological resistance in the form of defense mechanisms;
- Beside the inherited constitution of personality, one's development is determined by events in early childhood;

- Conflicts between conscious view of reality and unconscious (repressed) material can result in mental disturbances such as neurosis, neurotic traits, anxiety, depression etc.;
- The liberation from the effects of the unconscious material is achieved through bringing this material into the consciousness (via e.g. skilled guidance).

Even though these tenets are considered "pseudo-scientific" and much of the practice itself is no longer practiced in full, the basic foundations of psychotherapy are used by psychologists, psychiatrists, and counselors. Freud's understanding of the unconscious mind and the use of verbal treatment for psychopathology became the gold standard of practice for a number of years.

Sigmund Freud's theories have gone out of "vogue" within modern counseling and many attempts have been made to discredit him. Much of his work is distorted for this reason and the basic tenets of Freudian theory are, therefore, misunderstood. Below we are going to outline the basic tenets of Freudian theory and practice, that we may understand better what he taught and why he taught it.

- At the time of Freud's neurological studies (1885), the major form for neurological development was hypnosis. Freud himself studied under Jean-Martin Charcot, a renowned hypnotist. From this, Freud desired to develop a career in medical psychopathology rather than neurology.

- While treating a patient by the name of "Anna O," Freud learned the relevance in 'talk therapy." Freud drew on his inspiration for method from Josef Breuer, whose treatment of patients differed from other conventional methods of treatment at the time. While the patient was under hypnosis, Breuer would not encourage suggestions on the part of the hypnotist but encourage her to talk about her life and experiences as part of her therapy. He noted her symptoms started to subside, especially the more she spoke of her issues. Eventually Freud systemized this method of talk therapy, calling it "free association," to include dream analysis in addition to talking as a successful and systematic method of healing without hypnosis. His method of therapy became known as "psychoanalysis."

- The goal of Freudian psychoanalysis is to bring repressed thoughts, emotions, feelings, and memories to the surface, that by doing so, the patient may be healed from various psychological disorders.

- Freud's teachings centered largely around the unconscious mind and the various ways human beings manifested symptoms of repression. Within these theories included numerous other teachings about neurosis, mental illness, socialization, life, behavior, and the complexity of human actions.

- Freud taught that all human action was controlled by two drives: the life drive and the death drive. The life drive is the libido, which prompted survival, reproduction, thirst, hunger, and sex. The death drive is the principle by which something is reduced to nothingness.

- In Freudian theory, dreams represent the unconscious wishes and desires of a person, and they are encouraged to share as part of uncovering the unconscious mind. Freud first became a "household word" when he published his book, *The Interpretation of Dreams* in 1899.

- Freudian theory about infantile sexuality established human beings as sexual from birth. This arose from his work with numeral sexual abuse patients who reported memories of sexual abuse in childhood.

- Critical of religion, Freud believed religion was, at one time, necessary to control society's violent tendencies, but could now be abandoned in favor of science. With his position on religion, he often looked at it with a certain objectivity, seeing the repetition in many religious acts as having the potential to cause mental instability.

- Modern critics to Freud cite his use of cocaine in a modern sense. Freud was prescribed cocaine for ailments in his lifetime, as were most patients in the late 1800s and early 1900s. Cocaine was legal and prescribed for virtually every ailment known to man. It was Freud's analysis that first documented cocaine's effects on the body. Recognizing its dangers, Freud stopped using it, stopped prescribing it, and never recommended it again. It is worth noting, however, that had he not been the analyzer he was, it would have taken many more years for its dangers to be recognized.

Key Freudian terms

- **Ego:** The portion of the psyche that gives direction to the id; organized and realistic.

- **Id:** The completely unconscious portion of the psyche that operates by the pleasure principle, constantly seeking what feels good and is desirable to the individual. It is the source of human drives and a sense of immediate gratification; impulsive and instinctive.

- **Libido:** The "life drive." An unspecified driving force, often sexual in nature but not exclusively sexual. The libido develops in individuals by changing its object, moving through different sources of pleasure.

- **Oedipus complex:** Based on Sophocles' play *Oedipus Rex*, the Oedipus complex was a model of the need for constraint and discipline of sexuality. An Oedipus complex occurs when a child displays sexual interest in his mother or father to the exclusion of the other parent. The purpose in studying this belief was to point out that those driven to incest needed to control such an urge as well as instruct that adult sexuality and individuality are developed over time.

- **Psyche:** The human mind composed of both the conscious and unconscious parts.

- **Psychoanalysis:** The foundational technique used in all modern psychiatric analysis and counseling.

- **Psychosexual development:** The advance of an individual to live as a sexually healthy, functioning member of society. In Freudian theory, psychosexual development occurred over a number of years and was a part of the socialization of the individual. The stages of psychosexual development are the oral stage, the anal stage, the phallic stage, the latency phase, and the genital stage.

- **Socialization:** The process by which an individual is acclimated and becomes a member of a larger group of people, able to function and participate in life as part of the bigger picture of society. In Freudian theory, socialization comes about through stages of development and starts largely within the family unit or immediate environment.

- **Stages of development:** Freud's theory on developmental stages of development by which a child acclimates to society. The first stage is the oral stage of infancy, in which a child receives gratification through nursing. The second stage is the anal phase, by which a child receives gratification through toilet training and evacuating their bowels. The third stage is the phallic stage, by which children become aware of their genitals and their bodies; it is during this stage they develop an understanding of male and female and the basic differences therein. It is during the phallic stage that an Oedipus complex can arise. The fourth stage is the latency phase, starting anywhere from between three to seven years of age and lasting until between eight and thirteen years of age. It is an in-between phase, one of stability, in which the child identifies with their same-sex parent and the child begins to learn larger society's culture and values. It is during this period that a child can develop "infantile amnesia," or the repression of negative childhood memories, such as sexual abuse. The fifth stage of development is the genital stage, the onset of puberty, in which the sexual urges are directed at the opposite sex.

- **Sublimation:** A mature defense mechanism by which socially unacceptable impulses and drives are transformed into socially acceptable behaviors by an act of human will. It serves the greater whole of society through art or inventions.

- **Superego:** The "moral compass" of the psyche, composed often of outer voices and conscience instilled within an individual. It is critical and moralistic. The Superego serves to control the impulses and desires of the id. Most of an individual's actions are directed through the superego.

- **Transference:** The incidence whereby a patient directs feelings or thoughts toward a therapist or counselor that are rooted in feelings or thoughts towards other people in their lives.

Things to draw on from Freud's theories

- Verbalization of issues is essential for healing and success in counseling techniques. Patients must be encouraged to share for counseling or therapy to be successful.

- Sex is a dominant and driving force in the human condition. It is a mistake to think sex and sexual interaction are irrelevant in the interplay of human behavior.

- Impulses (sinful nature) can be controlled, contrary to modern teachings and thoughts on the topic.

- Socialization is essential for the growth and development of people within society. It is essential for all people to develop through different essential stages of growth to function productively in society and interact normally with their peers.

- Things kept repressed can hurt people's physical, mental, and emotional well-being.

Chapter Review

<u>Vocabulary</u>

Define the following words in 1-3 sentences.

- Psychotherapy
- Ego
- Id
- Libido
- Oedipus complex
- Psyche
- Psychoanalysis
- Psychosexual development
- Socialization
- Stages of development
- Sublimation
- Superego

<u>Character profiles</u>

Create an outline character sketch of the following figure in psychotherapy. Construct an outline on the life and work of the following individual.

- Sigmund Freud

<u>Infographic</u>

Create an infographic on the following:

- Freud's stages of development relating to psychosexual development

CARL JUNG

CHAPTER THREE

Carl Jung, Father of Analytical Psychology

I was looking in the visions in my mind as I lay on my bed, and behold,
an angelic watcher, a holy one, descended from heaven.
- Daniel 4:13

Carl Gustav Jung (1875-1961) is considered the father of analytical psychology. He was a Swiss psychiatrist who first saw the human psyche as religious in its nature and, therefore, in need of a spiritual examination. In connection with his theories, Jung spent much of his life investigating eastern and western philosophy and religion, alchemy, astrology, literature, art, and even occultism.

Jung wrestled with many issues in his early life, including a defining sense of patriarchy that emerged due to his mother's frequent bouts with mental instability. He believed her behavior was enveloped within a strange darkness of forces during night hours. He also took issue with his father's approach to faith, who was a minister, which was very intellectual and academic in theory and style. Jung was, himself, introverted and shy, and considered himself to have two personalities, much like his mother: one that lived in his modern times and another older, dignified, influential man with roots in an earlier time.

For six years, Freud and Jung worked closely as colleagues. As Jung developed more of his theories, however, Jung and Freud parted ways and became bitter adversaries. In contrast with Freudian theory which is very exact by nature, (Freud himself regarded Jung's interest in spirituality and occultism as unscientific), Jung's theories are very complex in their nature.

The essence of Jungian theory is about the development of individualization within a person, or the ability to become an individual. In contrast with Freudian theory which centered more on the individual's ability to become a part of society, Jung's theory centered more on the individual's pursuit of self-identity and awareness.

- Jung's theory of analytical psychology was unique to him, and served to promote his theories on the human mind. He believed that the unconscious mind was untouchable and unfathomable to genuine scientific research because it was unconscious, and therefore unobtainable.

- To be whole, Jung believed an 'awakening' of the psyche was necessary, which came about through the realization of Self. By bringing the unconscious elements to consciousness, the individual could begin the process of becoming individualized.

- Jung believed in a flow of psychic energy that operated through the psyche of all living beings. If the energy channel somehow was blocked, damaged, weak, or sick, that would affect the psyche negatively and could lead to an imbalance of harmony between the unconscious and the Self, resulting in neuroses.

- Jungian theory also delved into many areas of personality, analyzing how people can make decisions, as well as intelligence and different types of intelligence. Jungian theory operated in the abstract and tried to give a tangible method to the measures of intelligence and abstract understanding.

- Jung held to the belief that spiritual discovery was an essential part of the human experience and that people needed to develop spiritually to develop the full Self. For many years, Jung was a proponent of the belief that alcoholism could be cured if alcoholics developed a sense of spirituality in their lives.

- His interest and practice in the occult led many to believe he was more of a mystic than a scientist. Later in his life he wrote extensively on the relationship between psychiatry and alchemy and the archetype symbolism present in those who believed in UFOs and their imagery.

- Jung was a big advocate of individual rights in relationship to a person's native government. He saw government observances and flags, salutes, etc. as forms of spiritual idolatry.

Key Jungian terms

- **Anima:** The unconscious feminine component of man.

- **Animus:** The unconscious masculine component of a woman.

- **Archetype:** In Jungian theory, the ancient or archaic images that originate in and come from the collective unconscious. He also uses the term to refer to universal psychic dispositions that help implant the basic images and understanding within our unconscious. They were used to interpret observations and for dream analysis. Jung believed the number of archetypes in existence was limitless, but the most common ones simplified for use in Jungian theory are the persona, the anima, the animus, the great mother, the wise old man, the hero, and the self.

- **Collective unconscious:** Part of the unconscious mind that transcends humanity and all life forms with nervous systems. It describes how the psyche organizes experiences.

- **Complex:** A root pattern of feelings, thoughts, memories, understandings, and desires found in the personal unconscious mind. They are believed to be organized around a common theme. Complexes can be conscious, unconscious, or partially conscious and unconscious at the same time.

- **Extraversion:** The state of being in which one is preoccupied with obtaining gratification and pleasure outside of oneself. An extrovert is interested in human interaction, outgoing, talkative, assertive, and social.

- **Individuation:** The ability to become an individual with stability.

- **Introversion:** The state of being in which one is drawn inward, exceedingly preoccupied with one's own mental life. An introvert is more socially withdrawn and interested in solitary activities.

- **Myers-Briggs Type Indicator (MBTI):** A questionnaire designed to measure the way people approach things from a psychological perspective. This test was designed based on Jung's types and first published in 1921. Jung purposed there were two types of cognitive functions: rational functions, which are thinking and feeling, and irrational functions, which are sensing and intuition. These functions either operate in an introverted or an extroverted form. From there, an individual is assessed by type. There are sixteen possible combinations of 'types' that an individual can have based on the different dichotomies: Extraversion (E), Introversion (I), Sensing (S), Intuition (N), Thinking (T), Feeling (F), Judging (J), and Perception (P). The assessment is done as one answers questions based on the way they perceive or handle the world, and are then given an assessed letter combination. For example: ESTJ is "extroversion, sensing, thinking, judgment."

- **Neurosis:** In Jungian theory, neurosis results from a disruption in the harmony between the individual's unconsciousness, consciousness, and their higher self.

- **Persona:** A functional complex that masks the Ego and presents it to the world as an essential component of the psyche.

- **Personal unconscious:** A personal recollective database of experiences used to teach individual being.

- **Personality psychology:** The branch of psychology that studies personality and individual differentiations.

- **Self:** The regulating center of the psyche and the worker for the individualization of the person. As the regulating center, it represents everything unique, special, or differentiating about that individual person.

- **Shadow:** An unconscious complex consisting of the repressed, suppressed, or disliked qualities of a person's conscious self.

- **Synchronicity:** The occurrence of two unlikely events that are too unlikely or unrelated to happen at the same time.

- **Unconscious:** The processes of the mind that are not accessed by the consciousness.

- **Wise old man:** A symbolic personification of the wisdom of the Self.

Things to draw on from Jung's theories

- The personalities we have and the different dynamics we have within our personalities affect the way we view the world and our interactions with others.

- Knowing and having a relationship with God is essential to the healing of a person in totality: mind, body, soul, and spirit.

- The issues, ideas, and concepts we have, as well as the images we formulate within our minds, come from a variety of sources, including our upbringings and early backgrounds.

- People are complex and have many reasons for doing things that we may or may not easily understand.

- There is more to life and to understanding life than we can see on the surface.

Chapter Review

Vocabulary

Define the following words in 1-3 sentences.

- Analytical psychology
- Archetype
- Collective unconscious
- Complex
- Extraversion
- Introversion
- Myers-Briggs Type Indicator (MBTI)
- Neurosis
- Persona
- Personality psychology
- Self
- Unconscious
- Wise Old Man

Character Profiles

Create an outline character sketch of the following figure in psychotherapy. Construct an outline of the life and work of the following individual.

- Carl Jung

Project

Find a Myers-Brigg Type Indicator Test online and take it, reporting back what personality type you have.

- We recommend the one found at 16personalities.com, as it provides a thorough overview of the way this specific personality might manifest, what it might look like, and how such a personality might direct your interests, both personally and professionally, throughout life.

ALFRED ADLER

CHAPTER FOUR

Alfred Adler, Founder of the School of Individual Psychology

And do not be conformed to this world, but be transformed by the renewing of your mind,
so that you may prove what the will of God is, that which is good and acceptable and perfect.
- Romans 12:2

lfred Adler (1870-1937) was an Austrian doctor and psychotherapist who is considered the founder of the school of individual psychology. Along with Sigmund Freud, Adler was one of the core founders of the psychoanalytic movement. He was also the first major figure to break away from psychoanalysis and create his own independent schools of thought surrounding psychotherapy and personality. He went on to have a profound and lasting impact on counseling and psychotherapy. Along with Freud and Jung, Adler is considered one of the founders of depth psychology, which takes the unconscious mind into account in psychoanalytical assessment and research. Adler's basic theory of the human being was that each human person was an individuum, or an individual whole. He believed that the individual person was a part of or connected to their surrounding environment.

Individual psychology is the belief that each human individual is the best judge of his or her own needs, growth, desires, and interests. Rather than looking at motivating factors such as libido, which was core in Freudian understanding, Adler believed environmental factors played a key in human motivation. Adlerian theory can be broken down as follows:

- **The theory of compensation, defeat and over-compensation**[1]

According to Adler, an individual derives his personality traits from these essentially external factors. The character of the individual is formed by his responses to their influence in the following ways:

  - **Compensation**[2]

    Whenever a person suffers from any disadvantages that make him or her inferior to others, his or her main aim becomes to bring those disadvantages to an end. hose who are able to do this become successful in their lives on both social as well as individual bases.

  - **Resignation**[3]

    There are those who give in to their disadvantages and become reconciled to them. Such people are in the majority. The attitude of the world towards them is of a cool, rather uninterested sympathy.

  - **Over-compensation**[4]

    There are some persons who become so infatuated with the idea of compensating for their disadvantages that they end up over-indulging in the pursuit. These are the neurotics.

  Thus, the external factors are vital in character formation.

Adler's theories went far beyond practice and extended into issues of everyday living and application, such as birth order, parental and caregiver education, community, ecology, and metaphysical spirituality.

- Alfred Adler started out in ophthalmology and then switched to general practice. Many of his early patients were involved with the circus, and many of his later theories related to the anomalies present within the circus performers.

- He was an early part of the psychoanalytic movement, meeting with and working with Sigmund Freud. He would later break from this movement and started the Society for Individual Psychology in 1912. He was one of the first to disregard the psychiatrist's couch and, instead, meet with people face-to-face in two chairs. His work relates to bringing people into the here and now, examining the past so people can be constructive members of society.

- Much of his writing was for the public, rather than just for other doctors. His work has always had both professional and lay followers.

- Many of his theories have been picked up by neo-Freudians.

- Adler promoted holism, the belief that an individual should be treated as a whole, rather than compartmentalized by problems. This is social and community psychology as well as depth psychology. Adler advocated psychology as a preventative approach to problems and advocated the training of adults in child-oriented professions to learn ways to help children exercise power through making their own decisions.

- He was the first to argue from a feminist perspective in psychology, believing the power dynamics between men and women are an essential component in understanding the psychology of people.

- Adlerian practice follows in the following areas:[5]

- o Mental Health Prevention
- o Social Interest and Community Feeling
- o Holism and the Creative Self
- o Fictional Finalism, Teleology, and Goal constructs
- o Psychological and Social Encouragement
- o Inferiority, Superiority and Compensation
- o Lifestyle / Style of Life
- o Early Recollections (a projective technique)
- o Family Constellation and Birth Order
- o Life Tasks & Social Embeddedness
- o The Conscious and Unconscious realms
- o Private Logic & Common Sense (based in part on Kant's *sensus communis*)
- o Symptoms and Neurosis
- o Safeguarding Behavior
- o Guilt and Guilt Feelings
- o Socratic Questioning
- o Dream Interpretation
- o Child and Adolescent Psychology
- o Democratic approaches to Parenting and Families
- o Adlerian Approaches to Classroom Management
- o Leadership and Organizational Psychology

- Adlerian theory suggests personality operates as the unconscious works to convert feelings of inferiority to feelings of superiority. The desires a person has are checked and disciplined by societal morals and ethics.

- Adler agreed with Freud about the psychodynamic nature behind psychology but also maintained that human beings are guided by goals as well as an unknown "natural force."

- Adler believed strongly that the underlying force behind human behavior was aggression.

- Adlerian theory delves much into personality. There are four personality types: the Getting or Leaning type, the Avoiding type, the Ruling or Dominant type, and the Socially Useful type. Adler also delved deeply into birth order, believing that one's position as a child in the family affected their personality characteristics.

Key Adlerian terms

- **Avoiding type:** The personality type which avoids defeat, and, therefore, avoids risk taking and chances in life.

- **Birth order:** A theory of psychological personality profiling that dictates one's placement in their family's siblings affects their personality and human development. The purpose was to extend the relevance of life influence beyond mother and father. Adler believed firstborn children had the most favorable position, having the exclusive attention of parents, until the birth of a second child. The second-born child took attention away from the firstborn, causing them to feel "dethroned." Following a model of three children, the oldest child was most likely to have neurosis and addiction (because of excessive responsibility placed on an oldest child), youngest children would be overindulged and spoiled (having poor social empathy), and the middle child experiencing neither extreme, would fit well in society, but also, become a rebel.

- **Getting or leaning type:** The personality type which is selfish, taking without giving back. In Christian understanding, we would understand them to be people who reap, but do not sow

- **Inferiority complex:** A term used to indicate low self-esteem, or value, characterized by feelings of insecurity or negative evaluation when measured against someone else, in a person.

- **Personality disorders:** Adler's term for "neurotic character."

- **Psychodynamics:** The theory and systematic study of the various psychological forces that are found driving human behavior, especially the relation of consciousness to unconsciousness.

- **Ruling or dominant type:** The personality type that seeks power through control, manipulation, and anti-social behaviors.

- **Socially useful type:** The personality type which is outgoing, friendly, and sociable.

- **Teleology:** A philosophical concept about the presence of final causes existing in nature. In philosophy, technology also shows the same design and purpose in human action also exists in nature in a larger sense. Teleology is often applied to theory and ethics, as well.

Things to draw on from Adler's theories

- Aggression can work as a motivating factor, unto momentum.

- We can suppose we know what is best for somebody else, but people, as a rule, know what can be best for them (if they are operating within the parameters of sound judgment). We cannot judge other people based on what we think we would do in their situation or what would be best for them.

- Compensation, resignation, and over-compensation are all external factors that are a part of making up the whole of one's personality.

- People are a whole and need to be treated as such. We must avoid compartmentalizing people and identifying people as a diagnosis rather than as an individual.

- We need to be careful not to intimidate people in counseling, acting as if we are holding ourselves above the issues and problems they have. If counseling seeks to make people better members of society, we are their first contact with society in a healing context.

- Our work as counselors must be as practical as it is professional.

- It's important to look at the whole of an individual's past and present to measure their state. Don't make the mistake of over-exaggerating a relationship with one family member or relative over another.

- Different personality types cause different behaviors in people.

Chapter Review

<u>Vocabulary</u>

Define the following words in 1-3 sentences.

- Avoiding type
- Birth order
- Getting or leaning type
- Inferiority complex
- Psychodynamics
- Ruling or dominant type
- Socially useful type
- Teleology

<u>Character Profiles</u>

Create an outline character sketch of the following figure in psychotherapy. Construct an outline of the life and work of the following individual.

- Alfred Adler

<u>Slideshows</u>

Create two PowerPoint slideshows:

- One on Adler's theory of compensation, defeat, and over-compensation
- One on Adler's theory of birth order.

ABRAHAM MASLOW

CHAPTER FIVE

Abraham Maslow, Founder of Humanistic Psychology

Be of the same mind toward one another; do not be haughty in mind, but associate with the lowly.
Do not be wise in your own estimation.
- Romans 12:16

Abraham Harold Maslow (1908-1970) was an American professor of psychology and the founder of Maslow's hierarchy of needs. His work was part of the founding branch of psychology known as humanistic psychology, which seeks the betterment of the human person, believing people are basically good in their nature, approaching people holistically. The holistic approach of humanistic psychology incorporates meaning, values, freedom, disappointment, responsibility and accountability, human potential, spirituality, and Maslow's founding point, self-actualization.

Maslow lived as a Russian Jew, the child of immigrant parents, in Brooklyn, New York during days of common anti-Semitism. Dealing with this constant strife led to an overcoming spirit. Maslow also had a particular dislike for his mother and the values she lived by, which included prejudice and narcissism.

It was during World War II that Maslow's strong ethics on peace and a desire to heal the horrors of war led him to new psychological research on self-actualizing people. His writing contained many borrowed ideas from other psychologists, but he greatly expanded upon them with his own ideas. His work has continued to be relevant not just in psychiatry, but in religion, education, and business as well.

The basis of Maslow's theory is that human beings are basically good, despite the issues, evils, or problems they may have. His theories emphasized the need for people to be self-actualized, or consistent in their personality, as optimal for good health and life. Rather than focusing on the mentally ill, Maslow believed that all people should strive to live self-actualized lives.

- Maslow believed his theories were a compliment to Freud's theories – while Freud's work was for those who were mentally ill or sick, Maslow's theories pertained to healthy people, especially ways healthy people could become even better and more actualized in life.

- Maslow believed self-actualizing people have a coherent personality syndrome. To him, this was the ultimate in well-being and balance. Self-actualized people display the following traits[1]:

  o **Truth:** honest, reality, beauty, pure, clean and unadulterated completeness
  o **Goodness:** rightness, desirability, uprightness, benevolence, honesty
  o **Beauty:** rightness, form, aliveness, simplicity, richness, wholeness, perfection, completion,
  o **Wholeness:** unity, integration, tendency to oneness, interconnectedness, simplicity, organization, structure, order, not dissociated, synergy
  o **Dichotomy-transcendence:** acceptance, resolution, integration, polarities, opposites, contradictions
  o **Aliveness:** process, not-deadness, spontaneity, self-regulation, full-functioning
  o **Unique:** idiosyncrasy, individuality, non-comparability, novelty

- o **Perfection:** nothing superfluous, nothing lacking, everything in its right place, just-rightness, suitability, justice
- o **Necessity:** inevitability: it must be just that way, not changed in any slightest way
- o **Completion:** ending, justice, fulfillment
- o **Justice:** fairness, suitability, disinterestedness, non-partiality,
- o **Order:** lawfulness, rightness, perfectly arranged
- o **Simplicity:** nakedness, abstract, essential skeletal, bluntness
- o **Richness:** differentiation, complexity, intricacy, totality
- o **Effortlessness:** ease; lack of strain, striving, or difficulty
- o **Playfulness:** fun, joy, amusement
- o **Self-sufficiency:** autonomy, independence, self-determining

- Maslow believed that the way needs are met is just as important as meeting the needs. The combination of meeting needs and the way those needs are met defines human experience. This is how people reach out in interaction with other people, forming human connections.

- Maslow is best known for Maslow's hierarchy of needs, a visual aid created to detail his theory[2]:

  - o At the bottom of the pyramid are the "Basic needs or Physiological needs" of a human being, food and water and sex.
  - o The next level is "Safety Needs: Security, Order, and Stability." These two steps are important to the physical survival of the person. Once individuals have basic nutrition, shelter and safety, they attempt to accomplish more.
  - o The third level of need is "Love and Belonging," which are psychological needs; when individuals have taken care of

themselves physically, they are ready to share themselves with others, such as with family and friends.

o The fourth level is achieved when individuals feel comfortable with what they have accomplished. This is the "Esteem" level, the need to be competent and recognized, such as through status and level of success.

o Then there is the "Cognitive" level, where individuals intellectually stimulate themselves and explore.

o After that is the "Aesthetic" level, which is the need for harmony, order and beauty.

o At the top of the pyramid, "Need for Self-actualization," occurs when individuals reach a state of harmony and understanding because they have achieved their full potential. Once a person has reached the self-actualization state they focus on themselves and try to build their own image. They may look at this in terms of feelings such as self-confidence or by accomplishing a set goal.

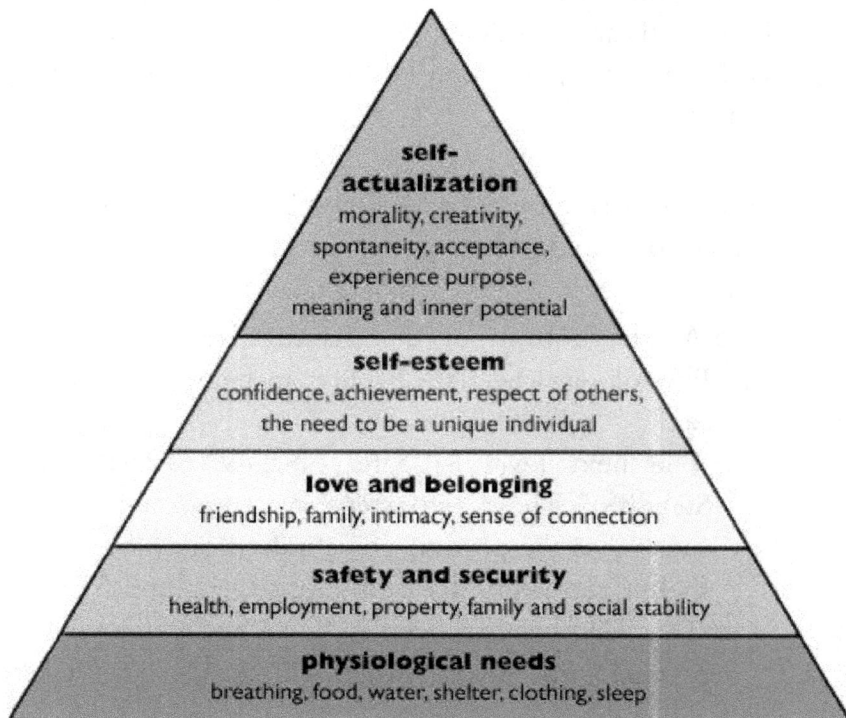

self-actualization
morality, creativity, spontaneity, acceptance, experience purpose, meaning and inner potential

self-esteem
confidence, achievement, respect of others, the need to be a unique individual

love and belonging
friendship, family, intimacy, sense of connection

safety and security
health, employment, property, family and social stability

physiological needs
breathing, food, water, shelter, clothing, sleep

- The first four levels of the hierarchy of needs are considered "D-needs,' or "Deficit Needs." This means if you don't have these first four levels of needs met, you will have a longing to have them met, and when you have them met, you will feel a sense of contentment. These needs, however, do not provide human motivation.

- Maslow believed that to meet needs, certain conditions had to be met, such as freedom of expression, speech, and search for information.

- One of Maslow's manners of thought is known as "being cognition" (b-cognition) which was in opposition to "deficit cognition" (d-cognition). The values of "being cognition" are known as "B-values." They are[3]:

  o **WHOLENESS** (unity; integration; tendency to one-ness; interconnectedness; simplicity; organization; structure; dichotomy-transcendence; order);
  o **PERFECTION** (necessity; just-right-ness; just-so-ness; inevitability; suitability; justice; completeness; "oughtness");
  o **COMPLETION** (ending; finality; justice; "it's finished"; fulfillment; finis and telos; destiny; fate);
  o **JUSTICE** (fairness; orderliness; lawfulness; "oughtness");
  o **ALIVENESS** (process; non-deadness; spontaneity; self-regulation; full-functioning);
  o **RICHNESS** (differentiation, complexity; intricacy);
  o **SIMPLICITY** (honesty; nakedness; essentiality; abstract, essential, skeletal structure);
  o **BEAUTY** (rightness; form; aliveness; simplicity; richness; wholeness; perfection; completion; uniqueness; honesty);
  o **GOODNESS** (rightness; desirability; oughtness; justice; benevolence; honesty);
  o **UNIQUENESS** (idiosyncrasy; individuality; non-comparability; novelty);

o **EFFORTLESSNESS** (ease; lack of strain, striving or difficulty; grace; perfect, beautiful functioning);

o **PLAYFULNESS** (fun; joy; amusement; gaiety; humor; exuberance; effortlessness);

o **TRUTH** (honesty; reality; nakedness; simplicity; richness; oughtness; beauty; pure, clean and unadulterated; completeness; essentiality).

o **SELF-SUFFICIENCY** (autonomy; independence; not-needing-other-than-itself-in-order-to-be-itself; self-determining; environment-transcendence; separateness; living by its own laws).

Key Maslow terms

- **Being-cognition:** Or "B-cognition," a state of awareness that is accepting and holistic.

- **Being values:** Or "B-values," the values associated with "B-cognition."

- **Coherent Personality Syndrome:** A consistent state of personality. In Maslow's theory, it is the optimal state of well-being, functioning, and psychological health.

- **Deficiency-cognition:** Or "D-cognition," a state of awareness that is the opposite of "B-cognition," noted by rejection and lack of wholeness.

- **Deficit-needs:** Or "D-needs," the first four levels of needs contained in Maslow's hierarchy of needs. They are such that, if a person is lacking one of them, they will seek out its fulfillment. The meeting of such needs leads to contentment.

- **Humanistic psychology:** A branch of psychology founded by Abraham Maslow, although the work of which was developed by many different psychologists, as well. It seeks to ensure a proper developmental process for optimal human functioning. The "self" of a person is given higher precedence, and the major focus is on the holism of the human person. It believes people are, despite behavior, basically good. Humanistic psychology draws on both religious and philosophical thought.

- **Maslow's hierarchy of needs:** Maslow's basic theory, often visualized as a pyramid, depicting the different basic and psychological needs human beings have: physiological, safety, love/belonging, esteem, and self-actualization.

- **Metamotivation:** A state of self-actualized people, who function in a drive motivated beyond basic needs. In Maslow's theory, this is how people develop their full capabilities.

- **Peak experiences:** High points in one's life noted by an individual's harmony within himself or herself and his or her surroundings. These may be major experiences or minor ones. Maslow believed that self-actualized people could have many of these experiences throughout the day, in contrast with others, who had them far less frequently.

- **Self-actualization**: The final and highest level of psychological achievement that is fulfilled when all other needs are met and the person is able to "actualize," or fully develop who they are.

Things to draw on from Maslow's theories

- There are basic needs within each human person: some are physical, some are psychological, and some pertain to a human being's potential. To meet higher needs, we cannot neglect basic needs, such as food, water, shelter, security, and morality.

- People cannot develop their potential if they do not have their needs met.

- How needs are met is just as relevant as meeting those needs themselves.

- Balance and consistency in human behavior is a sign of stability.

- People can need help at any stage of life, even people who are otherwise healthy and balanced. Reaching potential is not just for those who are mentally unstable or ill but is for everyone.

- Human connection and interaction is essential to the well-being of humanity.

- Because we are created in the image of God, goodness is a human quality. It may not be one everyone chooses to walk in, and it may very well be lost among many due to sin, but goodness is a part of our creation in God's image.

- People are a whole, and the whole aspect of every human person should be considered and valued.

Chapter Review

<u>Vocabulary</u>

Define the following words in 1-3 sentences.

- Being-cognition
- Being values
- Deficit-needs
- Humanistic psychology
- Maslow's hierarchy of needs
- Metamotivation
- Self-actualization

<u>Character Profiles</u>

Create an outline character sketch of the following figure in psychotherapy. Construct an outline on the life and work of the following individual.

- Abraham Maslow

<u>Infographic</u>

Create an infographic on:

- Maslow's hierarchy of needs.

KAREN HORNEY

CHAPTER SIX

Karen Horney, Co-Founder of the Neo-Freudian Discipline

And I set my mind to know wisdom and to know madness and folly;
I realized that this also is striving after wind.
- Ecclesiastes 1:17

K aren Danielsen Horney (1885-1952) was a German psychoanalyst who challenged Freud on his theories pertaining to sexuality and psychiatric orientation. For this reason, she is in a classification of theory known as Neo-Freudian.

Horney grew up in a strict environment, with her life dictated by her father's patriarchal values and morals. According to accounts, he was a cruel disciplinary figure who played favorites and favored her brother over her. Her mother was a softer counterpart, and more open-minded. As a result, Horney became attached to her mother more than her father. She was rebellious for a good part of her childhood, believing she'd never be attractive, so her better pursuit was spent on her mind. She also suffered from severe bouts of depression, which would follow her throughout her life. After her mother left her father, Horney enrolled in medical school with the support of her mother and the lack thereof from her father. Her pursuit of education rates her the reputation of a pioneer for women in psychoanalysis; she enrolled in medical school (1906) six years after the University of Freiburg began admitting women. Her married life (married to Oskar Horney in 1909) proved unhappy and, in many ways, to be a repeat of her childhood for her own children. Horney eventually left her husband after his severe bout with illness and another severe bout of hers of depression. She took herself and her children to Brooklyn, New York, continuing to practice psychotherapy for the rest of her life.

Karen Horney's work drew on earlier theories, especially those of Sigmund Freud, but approached several issues from a radically different viewpoint or expanded upon them in many ways. This has caused her to be a co-founder (along with Alfred Adler) of the Neo-Freudian discipline.

- Karen Horney viewed neurosis differently than others in her day. In her day, neurosis was believed to be a negative response to something external, such as trauma or abuse. She believed neurosis to be a continued process, with evidence of neurosis to be displayed throughout a person's lifetime.

- She emphasized parental indifference toward a child, believing a child or person's perception of an event was more relevant than the intentions of the person who was behind the event.

- Horney identified ten patterns of neurotic needs, based upon things needed for all human beings to be successful and balanced in life. A neurotic could display all the needs, or only some of them. They are, as follows[1]:

  o **Moving toward people**

    1. The need for affection and approval; pleasing others and being liked by them.
    2. The need for a partner; one whom they can love and who will solve all problems.

  o **Moving against people**

3. The need for power; the ability to bend wills and achieve control over others—while most persons seek strength, the neurotic may be desperate for it.
4. The need to exploit others; to get the better of them. To become manipulative, fostering the belief that people are there simply to be used.
5. The need for social recognition; prestige and limelight.
6. The need for personal admiration; for both inner and outer qualities—to be valued.
7. The need for personal achievement; though virtually all persons wish to make achievements, as with No. 3, the neurotic may be desperate for achievement.

- o **Moving away from people**

8. The need for self-sufficiency and independence; while most desire some autonomy, the neurotic may simply wish to discard other individuals entirely.
9. The need for perfection; while many are driven to perfect their lives in the form of well-being, the neurotic may display a fear of being slightly flawed.
10. Lastly, the need to restrict life practices to within narrow borders; to live as inconspicuous a life as possible.

- Horney condensed her ten needs into three broad categories:

  - o **Compliance:** A process of moving towards people, known as self-effacement. They often seek admiration or affirmation from peers. This is the combined category for needs one and two.

  - o **Aggression:** Needs three through seven fall under the category of "aggression." People in this category exhibit anger and aggressive behaviors, as they have a need for power, control, and exploitation. They too may seek recognition among their peers, but not in the sense of affirmation — more in a sense of commanding presence or authority. They are often self-centered and keep other people away.

- o **Detachment:** The category for needs eight through ten. Detached individuals seek self-sufficiency, having never received attention through neediness or aggressive means in childhood. They often seek solitude and perfection and repress feelings of love or hate for others.

- In contrast to Freud and many other psychiatrists at the time, Horney believed narcissism to be a personality development based on environmental conditions crossing with certain kinds of temperament or disposition. She believed narcissism resulted from indulgence, rather than lack of attention or met needs. She did not believe narcissists had high self-esteem, however, because they did not ever earn things themselves, nor feel the sense of self-accomplishment.

- Horney also took issue with Freud's theory of "penis envy," which theorizes women are jealous of men's power in the world. Horney did assert that while some women may experience this, "womb envy" was just as common an occurrence in men. She also re-worked the Oedipus Complex, believing the root of such was anxiety. Despite her few disagreements with Freudian theory, she adhered to Freudian belief, and sought to make it applicable in a holistic, whole-person approach and sense.

- Like Abraham Maslow, Karen Horney believed self-actualization to be something to which all people strive. In contrast with neurosis, self-actualization is a healthy part of a person's life. A person can have two views of their self: the real self, which is who they really are, and the ideal self, which is who the individual thinks they should be. A neurotic person is split between their real self and their idealized self.

- As a pioneer of feminine psychiatry, Horney was the first woman to present a paper on female psychiatry. Through her work, she proved women were encouraged by their cultures and the regulations therein to be dependent upon men, for love, finances, and status. In this pursuit, men were overvalued, and women were undervalued as objects of beauty or charm, thereby unable to achieve self-actualization. She wrote that women, according to traditional values, were only able to gain value through children and, by extension, family. If a husband-wife relationship follows traditional patterns, it could lead to neurosis, as the roles mimic that of parent and child. She believed both men and women had a drive toward productivity and intelligence, and that women need to satisfy this drive. In her theory, women often seek to meet this need through childbirth, while men strive to accomplish much in a given field — thereby, proof of an over-compensation as they are unable to bear children.

Key Horney terms

- **Basic anxiety:** The fear of helplessness or abandonment, which occurs when the needs found under the category of "compliance" are not met.

- **Expansive solution:** Karen Horney's three "neurotic" solutions; a three-part combination of narcissistic, perfectionist, and arrogant-vindictive approaches to life.

- **Feminine psychology:** Psychology about and from the perspective of women. As psychoanalysis and psychology were often pioneered and theories were authored by men, feminine psychology balances the often male-dominated perspectives with female perspectives on the mind, life, family, and mental states. Karen Horney was a pioneer in feminine psychology.

- **Neo-Freudianism:** A group of loosely connected psychologists and psychologists whose theories, writings, and beliefs pertaining to psychology were largely influenced by Sigmund Freud. They either changed or, more often, expounded upon Freudian theory in their own works and practices. Karen Horney and Alfred Adler are considered the co-founders of Neo-Freudian discipline.

- **Resignation:** One's detachment from other people.

- **Self:** In Horney's theory, the essence of one's being and potential.

- **Self-effacement:** A submission or reduction of oneself to other people.

- **Ten patterns of neurotic needs:** The needs of neurotic people, either in whole or in part, that form the basis of universal human need for success and balance in life. They are further divided into three categories: compliance (moving toward people), aggression (behaving with aggressive tendencies toward others) and detachment (self-sufficiency and isolation).

- **Womb envy:** The male counterpart to Freudian penis envy, womb envy is the belief that men are envious of a woman's ability to bear children and, the associated connection with it, that women can give life. In conjunction with womb envy, a man will drive himself to create incredible inventions, a sign of over-compensation.

Things to draw on from Horney's theories

- The way people perceive an event, a behavior, or an action on the part of another is more relevant than the intention of that action.

Perception, even though it may not reflect reality, is very key to how people perceive life in general.

- Neurosis is not something that may be limited to a continual state of being but may be something a person experiences more than once in their lifetime.

- To be successful and balanced in life, we all have needs that must be met. The absence of a need can be problematic, and we must, as counseling professionals, examine the issue at hand to resolve the problem a person may be having.

- Narcissism is not always present due to lack but can just as easily exist due to over-indulgence.

- To truly develop self-esteem, one must accomplish things for themselves.

- People need to develop themselves and should be encouraged to become everything they seek and strive to become.

- The dynamics between men and women must be considered in psychology. The issues women face, the way they perceive an feel about them, and the way a woman is treated by her family and society should all be considered when it comes to a woman's mental state or emotional difficulties. Women must be encouraged to achieve, rather than accept a menial or subordinate position. Women's contributions to various matters are just as relevant as a man's contributions and should never be treated as having a diminished relevance.

Chapter Review

Vocabulary

Define the following words in 1-3 sentences.

- Basic anxiety
- Feminine psychology
- Neo-Freudianism
- Resignation
- Self
- Self-effacement
- Ten patterns of neurotic needs
- Womb envy

Short Answer

Answer the following question in 1 to 3 sentences.

- How was Karen Horney's work on feminine psychology innovative, and why was it important?

Character Profiles

Create an outline character sketch of the following figure in psychotherapy. Construct an outline on the life and work of the following individual.

- Karen Horney

Slideshows

Create a PowerPoint slideshow on:

- Horney's ten patterns of neurotic needs.

MELANIE KLEIN

CHAPTER SEVEN

Melanie Klein, Founder of Play Therapy

The mind of the intelligent seeks knowledge,
But the mouth of fools feeds on folly.
- Proverbs 15:14

Melanie Riezes Klein (1882-1960) was a Austrian-born, British psychoanalyst who developed therapeutic techniques for use with children. She was a leader and pioneer in the work of object relations theory, a description of the way the psyche develops in response to others in an environment.

Klein's work began with her own experiences in psychotherapy: she was the patient. She started analyzing children in Budapest in 1919. Two of her first patients were possibly her own son and daughter. In 1921 she worked in Berlin, not finding a great deal of support for her work, and later, she went to Britain, where she worked until her death in 1960.

When Freud and, subsequently, Freudian theory came to Britain in 1938, a division emerged over theory and practice. To this day, the British Psychoanalytical Society is divided into three groups: Kleinian, Anna Freudian, and Independent. The first group, Kleinian, follows the theories and practice of Melanie Klein. Her work is very well-known in Britain, and very influential on British psychoanalysis. She is also a predominant psychiatric force in Latin America and Europe, as a whole. This is especially noteworthy as she did not hold a college degree and was a divorced woman in a predominately man's game. Her life was difficult, complete with issues from childhood until her death, including sibling deaths, the death of her son, career interruption due to marriage and family, and estrangement from her daughter.

- Though Melanie Klein challenged some Freudian theories (including the timing of the Oedipus complex and his teaching on the timing of the superego), she always considered herself faithful to Freudian concept and technique. She was the first to use traditional psychoanalysis techniques for children.

- Klein's work was innovative in technique. She was the first to incorporate play with toys into psychoanalysis, in a field now known as "play therapy." This arose from her belief that play was the main outlet for emotional communication with children. She would watch them play with assorted toys and interpret the purpose behind the interaction. She is also known for her teachings on infant development.

- Klein believed aggression to be an important force when analyzing children. This was a different perspective from other popular theorists, including Freud's daughter, Anna Freud.

- Her theoretical work incorporates Freud's theory of "death instinct," the belief that all living things are drawn to an inorganic, or inactive, state (i.e., death). This contrasts with the life principle. Life Freud, Klein believed these two principles to be the basis for the psyche. She also believed in the development and existence of the id, ego, and superego.

- After watching severely disturbed and ill children, Klein proposed a new model of the human psyche: the psyche would oscillate back and forth between life and death principles. When the life principle was in the forefront, it was known as the depressive position. Her theories on the state of being focused on the inorganic state of being paranoid-schizoid position.

- Adult psychiatric treatment within the Kleinian school is much like that of traditional psychoanalysis, using a couch, and focusing on deep early emotions and fantasies.

Key Kleinian terms

- **Controversial discussions:** A series of scientific meetings of the British Psychoanalysis Society between the supporters of Kleinian theory and the Vienna school of thought, largely headed up by Anna Freud. The result of these discussions was the tri-part division of the British Psychoanalysis Society: Anna Freudian, Kleinian, and Independent.

- **Depressive position:** In Kleinian theory, the state of the psyche when the principle of life (as opposed to death) is the dominant force, or factor.

- **Object relations theory:** A description of the development of the psyche as dependent on environment. The basis of the theory is that the way we interact and relate with others as adults was programmed within us by the way we interacted with our parents as infants. The Self (or subject) relates to different Objects (images, ideas, or concepts) in the unconscious mind, and can influence us throughout life. It is the concept of subconscious association – the way we interact with something associated with something from childhood can impact how we interact with others throughout our lives.

- **Play therapy:** A therapeutic method used on children between the ages of three and eleven using natural play as a technique to help them through a healing process. It is compared to the same "free association" technique used in adults.

- **Paranoid-schizoid position:** In Kleinian theory, the state of the psyche when the principle of death (as opposed to life), in a disintegrating tendency, is the dominant force, or factor.

Things to draw on from Klein's theories

- Children are not adults, and the way children are counseled must be on a comfortable level and familiar to children. Play therapy has proven effective and relevant for children, as it helps them to remain comfortable and grounded during analysis and treatment.

- Play largely explains and shows how children view the world. Never underestimate the revelation and "emotional speech" present through a child's play.

- People can switch between varied states of mind and being, depending on their circumstances, feelings, or the forces of life at play. In Christian counseling, we would understand this concept to speak on the level of an individual being in a state of mind that is carnal (death) or a state of mind that is life (Christ). Just because one is saved or claims to be such does not mean they have fully put on the mind of Christ and does not mean they do not wrestle with the thoughts of carnality.

Chapter Review

Vocabulary

Define the following words in 1-3 sentences.

- Controversial discussions
- Depressive position
- Object relations theory
- Play therapy
- Paranoid-schizoid position

Short Answer

Answer the following questions in 1 to 3 sentences each.

- Melanie Klein's integration of toys and play into therapy was innovative for her time. Why was this work important, and how does it benefit us today?
- Describe Melanie Klein's Object Relations Theory and how it differs from other psychoanalytical thoughts.

Character Profiles

Create an outline character sketch of the following figure in psychotherapy. Construct an outline of the life and work of the following individual.

- Melanie Klein

ERICH FROMM

CHAPTER EIGHT

Erich Fromm, Psychologist, Psychoanalyst, and Philosopher

Set your mind on the things above, not on the things that are on earth.
- Colossians 3:2

Erich Seligmann Fromm (1900-1980) was a German psychologist, psychoanalyst, philosopher, and sociologist. He is often best-known for his involvement with a group that later became known as the Frankfurt School of Critical Theory, which examined life and culture across the various aspects of the humanities. He is known for his broad-spectrum contributions to psychiatry, psychology, sociology, and philosophy.

Erich Fromm was born in Frankfurt am Main, as the only son to his Orthodox Jewish parents. In college, he trained in sociology and later worked in psychoanalysis. He left Germany after the Nazi invasion, and lived in Geneva, Switzerland, followed by Brooklyn, New York. While in Brooklyn, he had a personal relationship with Karen Horney, and they had a marked influence on the one another's thoughts and theories. Fromm would go on to work for several colleges, teaching and helping to establish psychiatric departments in many universities throughout the world.

- Fromm's view of the world came from his study of the Talmud, the Jewish law under Rabbinical Judaism. Even though he turned away from religion to pursue secular ideas, his foundation of Talmudic roots underlined his world view.

- The foundation to Fromm's humanistic philosophy is found in Fromm's understanding about Adam and Eve, rooted in much of his Talmudic understanding. Rather than seeing Adam and Eve's eating from the Tree of Knowledge as a bad thing, he lauds them for independent action and establishing their own moral values rather than relying on authoritarian values. From there, Fromm analyzes the story of Adam and Eve from the perspective of biological evolution and human angst, becoming aware of their own mortality. He believed that guilt and shame arise from the realization of a disunified humanity. The solution to guilt and shame is to develop love and reason.

- Love was a key point of Fromm's theory. He believed in love to be a creative force and capacity rather than just a human emotion. Spanning an understanding of love, Fromm believed love was more than falling in love or selfish understandings of it. He truly believed the common elements of love are care, responsibility, respect, and knowledge. He used the Biblical Prophet Jonah (who did not want to go and preach repentance to the Ninevites) as an example to display genuine care and responsibility are lacking in most human relationships. As part of love, human beings need to respect the autonomy of one another.

- Fromm also wrote extensively on freedom, believing it is a part of human experience that one either tries to escape from or tries to embrace. He believed embracing freedom of will within ourselves to be a healthy thing, while escaping freedom was the root of psychological conflict. Fromm outlined three escape mechanisms: automation conformity (changing one's ideal self to conform to society's ideal personality type), authoritarianism (giving one's control to another), and destructiveness (any process that attempts to eliminate others or the entire world).

- From theorized human beings have eight basic needs[1]:

  o **Relatedness:**
  Relationships with others, care, respect, knowledge.

  o **Transcendence:**
  Being thrown into the world without their consent, humans must transcend their nature by destroying or creating people or things. Humans can destroy through malignant aggression, or killing for reasons other than survival, but they can also create and care about their creations.

  o **Rootedness:**
  Rootedness is the need to establish roots and to feel at home again in the world. Productively, rootedness enables us to grow beyond the security of our mother and establish ties with the outside world. With the nonproductive strategy, we become fixated and afraid to move beyond the security and safety of our mother or a mother substitute.

  o **Sense of identity:**
  The drive for a sense of identity is expressed nonproductively as conformity to a group and productively as individuality.

  o **Frame of orientation:**
  Understanding the world and our place in it.

  o **Excitation and stimulation:**
  Actively striving for a goal rather than simply responding.

- **Unity:**
  A sense of oneness between one person and the "natural and human world outside."

- **Effectiveness:**
  The need to feel accomplished.

- Fromm also taught that there were six orientations of character, which mark how an individual interacts with the outside world. The six orientations emerge from two ways in which people relate to the world: assimilation (acquiring things) and socialization (interactions and reactions to others). These six orientations are Receptive, Explorative, Hoarding, Necrophilous, Marketing, and the one positive orientation, Productive. The four non-productive orientations were validated by a psychometric test, The Person Relatedness Test, between 1953 and 1955.

Key Fromm terms

- **Authoritarianism:** Giving of one's control to another.

- **Automation conformity:** Changing one's ideal self to conform the self to society's idea of the ideal personality.

- **Biophila hypothesis:** The belief that there is a distinctive connection between human beings and all other living systems. The word literally means "love of life or living systems." This term was first used by Erich Fromm to describe an orientation of being drawn to all that is alive and vital.

- **Destructiveness:** Any process that attempts to eliminate other people from the world or the world as a whole.

- **Eight basic needs:** Eric Fromm's theory of the essential needs of human beings: relatedness, transcendence, rootedness, sense of identity, frame of orientation, excitation and stimulation, unity, and effectiveness.

- **Love:** In Fromm's theories, love was not an emotion, but an interpersonal and creative capacity. He believed that what we perceive as true love is, indeed, narcissistic and sado-masochistic. True love always holds the keys of care, respect, responsibility, and knowledge.

- **Six orientations:** Six orientations of character which marks how an individual interacts with the outside world. The six orientations emerge from two ways in which people relate to the world: assimilation (acquiring things) and socialization (interactions and reactions to others). These six orientations are Receptive, Explorative, Hoarding, Necrophilous, Marketing, and Productive.

- *The Art of Loving*: Erich Fromm's most famous book, an international bestseller first published in 1956. This book reemphasized many of Fromm's earlier thoughts and principles.

Things to draw on from Fromm's theories

- Spiritual understanding needs to influence the way we view the world and the way we handle our patients as Christian counselors.

- Love needs to be taught and pursued as more than just a nice, emotional musing: it needs to be something tangible that creates life. Love needs to be more than a selfish or fairy tale concept in our counseling practices; it needs to be something visible, tangible, and changes people's lives.

- If we, as Christian counselors, believe in freedom in Christ, we must be attuned to legalistic tendencies in people that cause them to run from freedom. There is an essential relevance to identify psychological ways people try to run from freedom in Christ.

- Fromm's eight basic needs must be considered when people deal with problems and addressed with positive solutions.

- There are several different ways a person may interact with the outside world, and we must be aware of those differences.

Chapter Review

<u>Vocabulary</u>

Define the following words in 1-3 sentences.

- Authoritarianism
- Automation conformity
- Biophila hypothesis
- Destructiveness
- Eight basic needs
- Love
- Six orientations
- The Art of Loving

<u>Short Answer</u>

Answer the following questions in 1 to 3 sentences each.

- How did Erich Fromm's Jewish childhood impact his theories and his philosophies?
- In Fromm's theory, how does love change the world? How is the principle, as found herein, relevant to the Christian believer?

<u>Character Profiles</u>

Create an outline character sketch of the following figure in psychotherapy. Construct an outline of the life and work of the following individual.

- Erich Fromm

<u>Infographic</u>

Create an infographic on:

- Fromm's eight basic needs.

B.F. SKINNER

CHAPTER NINE

B.F. Skinner, Founder of Radical Behaviorism

I explored with my mind how to stimulate my body with wine while my mind was guiding me wisely,
and how to take hold of folly, until I could see what good there is for the sons of men to do under heaven
the few years of their lives.
- Ecclesiastes 2:3

Burrhus Frederic Skinner (1904-1990) was a American behaviorist, philosopher, author, and inventor. He is the founder of radical behaviorism, which believes all living action is determined, and not free. It is considered anti-theoretical, in contrast to most other psychological and psychoanalytical practices.

Skinner was born in Susquehanna, Pennsylvania. He became an atheist after a liberal Christian instructor tried to deter his fear of hell, which had been instilled within him by his grandmother. His original pursuit was in writing but soon found that he was not interested in writing as a career.

It was his encounter with John Watson's (1878-1958) theories on Behaviorism (as Watson established the theory) that sparked an interest in Skinner. Behaviorism is a psychological philosophy based in the theory that all living beings (including the abstract such as thinking or feeling and the non-abstract) should be regarded as behaviors. In the instance of psychological issues, behavior or environment should be changed to correct the problem. Behaviorism believes that all behavior can be described scientifically, without thought or consideration to psychological understandings, events, or even hypothesis surrounding the mind. They believe that all public action is the same, with no philosophical difference, to private action, such as thinking. The main influence behind the Behaviorist movement was Ivan Pavlov (1849-1956), a Russian physiologist who is best known for his experiment involving "Pavlov's dogs." Pavlov would use various methods to signal it was time to feed the dogs, and upon seeing, hearing, or feeling one of those methods (often spoken of as a bell, but it is inconclusive whether Pavlov used a bell), the dogs would salivate in anticipation of eating. Skinner's Behaviorism is known as "Radical Behaviorism," believed to be the science of behavior. Its purpose is to understand behavior as a function of environmental conditioning based on the reinforcement of consequences, be those consequences positive or negative. This creates a system whereby behavior can be produced. Unlike other systems of Behaviorism, Radical Behaviorism denies personal actions, such as thinking, feeling, perceptions, and observations as part of the reasoning behind the behavior of living things.

- Skinner believed that behavior is maintained from one situation or condition to another through similar or the same consequences (be they positive or negative) for actions. In other words, Radical Behaviorism theorizes that behaviors are casual by-standards of consequences.

- Consequences can be positive or negative and should be regarded as concepts of reinforcement. They work to ensure behavior will occur again.

- Skinner believed his theory applied to all living organisms, not just to people.

- Radical Behaviorism believes that the consequence of an action reinforces behavior over time, rather than a single action of consequence at a given time. The theory states there is a schedule of reinforcement: continuous reinforcement (done at every occurrence of the behavior), interval (fixed/variable) reinforcement (a fixed reinforcement follows after the first response following a pause in time, while a variable reinforcement means the time that goes by before consequence comes is not set, but varies around an average time frame), and ratio (fixed/variable) reinforcement (a fixed reinforcement indicates a set number of responses occur before there is reinforcement, while a variable reinforcement indicates there must be a number of responses delivered before reinforcement, it is different from the last, but has an average value).

- Skinner's work in Radical Behaviorism led to many of his own inventions, all of which related to his theories on behavior. Some of these inventions were very controversial, including the air crib (a box designed to aid in the raising of children that was easy to clean and temperature and humidity controlled), the operant conditioning chamber (also called the "Skinner box," designed as an experiment box with pellets dispensed for reward success), cumulative recorder (an instrument used to automatically document behavior), and a teaching machine (a mechanical object used to automate a set curriculum instruction).

- Skinner's Radical Behaviorism affected education as well as the world of psychology. In Behaviorist perspective, education has only two purposes: teaching areas of verbal and non-verbal behavior and encourage students to display an interest in learning. He believed students could be controlled in their behavior when certain stimulation was present. He believed that teachers needed to change their approach, rewarding positive behavior more than reinforcing punishment for negative behavior. He believed the main thing people learned from punishment was how to avoid punishment in the future. In his book, *The Technology of Teaching*, he breaks down why he believes teachers fail[1]:

o Using aversive techniques (which produce escape and avoidance and undesirable emotional effects);
o Relying on telling and explaining ("Unfortunately, a student does not learn simply when he is shown or told." p. 103);
o Failing to adapt learning tasks to the student's current level;
o Failing to provide positive reinforcement frequently enough.

- On the reverse, Skinner believed any skill can be taught if it is done in an age appropriate manner[2]:

  o Clearly specify the action or performance the student is to learn to do.
  o Break down the task into small achievable steps, going from simple to complex.
  o Let the student perform each step, reinforcing correct actions.
  o Adjust so that the student is always successful until finally the goal is reached.
  o Transfer to intermittent reinforcement to maintain the student's performance.

Key Skinner terms

- **Behaviorism:** A psychological philosophy based in the theory that all living beings (including the abstract such as thinking or feeling and the non-abstract) should be regarded as behaviors. In the instance of psychological issues, behavior or environment should be changed to correct the problem. Behaviorism believes that all behavior can be described scientifically, without thought or consideration to psychological understandings, events, or even hypothesis surrounding the mind. They believe that all public action is the same, with no philosophical difference, to private action, such as thinking. The main foundational resource for Behaviorism is Ivan Pavlov (1849-1956), and the belief system was established and popularized by John Watson (1878-1958).

- **Continuous reinforcement:** In the schedules of reinforcement, the conditioned response is done at every occurrence of a behavior.

- **Interval (fixed/variable) reinforcement:** In the schedules of reinforcement, the two options: a fixed reinforcement follows the first response following a pause in time, while a variable reinforcement means the time that goes by before consequence comes is not set but varies around an average time frame). Both see the conditioned consequence come forth, but at an interval of response, rather than a regular interval of response.

- **Radical behaviorism:** The science of behavior founded by B.F. Skinner. Its purpose is to understand behavior as a function of environmental conditioning based on the reinforcement of consequences, regardless of whether those consequences are positive or negative. This creates a system whereby behavior is produced. Unlike other systems of Behaviorism, Radical Behaviorism denies personal actions, such as thinking, feeling, perceptions, and observations as part of the reasoning behind the behavior of living things.

- **Ratio (fixed/variable) reinforcement:** In the schedules of reinforcement, the two options: a fixed reinforcement indicates a set number of responses occur before there is reinforcement, while a variable reinforcement indicates there must be several responses delivered before reinforcement, it is different from the last but has an average value. In both instances, the conditioned reinforcement comes at an erratic interval, without consistency.

- **Schedules of reinforcement:** The theory that the consequence of an action reinforces behavior over time, rather than a single action of consequence at a given time. The theory states there is a schedule of reinforcement: continuous reinforcement, interval (fixed/variable) reinforcement and ratio (fixed/variable) reinforcement.

Things to draw on from Skinner's theories

- The way we treat people can impact their behavior. We do not want to be people who reward negative behavior and ignore positive behavior. We must be careful as to our responses to people, to ensure we are not reinforcing undesirable behavior within them.

- Never underestimate the role of conditioning in someone's life. Many behaviors can be changed if people are willing to change their behavior.

- Teachers should ensure their actions and methods are age-appropriate and instructions are clear within an age-appropriate manner.

Chapter Review

Vocabulary

Define the following words in 1-3 sentences.

- Behaviorism
- Radical Behaviorism
- Continuous reinforcement
- Interval (fixed/variable) reinforcement
- Ratio (fixed/variable) reinforcement
- Schedules of reinforcement

Short Answer

Answer the following questions in 1 to 3 sentences each.

- How has Skinner's radical behaviorism changed the face of the United States through education, child-rearing, and life in general? What are some other examples of behaviorism's influence on culture at large?

Character Profiles

Create an outline character sketch of the following figure in psychotherapy. Construct an outline on the life and work of the following individual.

- B.F. Skinner

Essay Questions

Construct a well-written essay (minimum 5-8 sentences), answering the following question.

<u>Infographic</u>

Create an infographic on:

- Skinner's schedules of reinforcement

CHAPTER TEN

The Failures in Modern Christian Counseling…and the Solution

Therefore, prepare your minds for action, keep sober in spirit,
fix your hope completely on the grace to be brought to you at the revelation of Jesus Christ.
- 1 Peter 1:13

The modern concept of Christian counseling dates back to 1970, when a man by the name of Jay E. Adams (1929-2020) wrote a book criticizing the use of psychological technique by Christians. He believed the Bible alone was sufficient for Christian counseling and started his own technique and organization surrounding that understanding. Christians were discouraged from learning more about psychological and psychiatric movements, citing them as "worldly" and "evil." One of the primary techniques used to discredit the modern movement was to criticize the founders of those movements and their personal spiritual beliefs.

The result of this push has been the creation of hundreds of different counseling schools and techniques, all believed to be founded upon the Bible, or more relevantly, built upon the founder's concept of what is Biblical. In this maze of a world of "Christian counseling," we have seen more disagreement, more disharmony, and numerous denominational concepts about counseling imposed on seeking people. Overall, the Christian counseling genre has been a total failure, for a few reasons. Not only are people not being helped, the warping of the Bible as well as the foundations of psychoanalytical theory have created a confused church, a damaged people, and an unhealthy Christian population: mentally, physically, emotionally, and yes, even spiritually. If, as believers we are called to "know them by their fruits" (Matthew 7:16-20), the "fruit" of modern Christian counseling is an evil upon the Body of Christ.

What many do not realize is the foundation to modern Christian counseling is not the Bible, but a cross between the Behaviorism of John Watson and the Radical Behaviorism of B.F. Skinner. In other words, the methods of Christian counseling are based in the theories of an atheist – conditioning behavior and changing behavior – not in Scripture. While Christian counselors have made many strides to try and make any strain of Behaviorism of divine principle, they cannot. The Bible and its various people, societies, cultures, issues, and thoughts prove that people are more than environmental conditioning. If we believe the human person to be composed of soul, spirit, and body, there is no way any of us can believe the precept of human counseling and the healing of human ills is as simple as re-conditioning human behavior. If such was true, the law would have been sufficient to save humanity (Acts 7:53, Romans 2:23). As we know it was not (Isaiah 24:5, Romans 3:28, Romans 4:15, Romans 6:14-15, Romans 9:31), this means people are deeper than mere behavioral conditioning. We can't "program" people to be Christian, nor to be mentally stable, nor to be the way we want them to be. There is more to the human person than behavioral reinforcement. We have choices, we have issues, we have thoughts and feelings, and the true call of the Christian counselor will uphold all of these when approaching the importance of Christian counseling.

The flawed theology of modern Christian counseling

Despite the different strains of Christian counseling, most Christian counseling can be summarized very simply. Modern Christian counseling, based in a fundamentalist approach rather than a Spirit-based theology. It is about the dryness of a text, the limited understanding and various interpretations of Christian thought, rather than understanding human issues. As with behaviorism, there are two essential components missing: human empathy and human understanding.

In modern Christian counseling theory, sin is the ailment of everything. Tracing sin back to the fall of humankind, sin gets the bad rap for all the problems people have: every mental illness, every emotional problem, breakdowns in relationships, and the like – are all the fault of sin. The theory is to bring people to Christ and then get them to stop sinning. In Christian counseling, sinful behavior is seen as a conditioned response, something to control, rather than a human condition. It is believed that with a lot of prayer, talk, Bible reading, and supernatural powers that a person can control every sinful impulse they have.

While I do believe the root of human ailment is sin – because, as sin entered the world, so did the consequences of sin – I do not believe that sin is a conditioned response. Sin is a part of being a human being. It is something all do, as all fall short of the glory of God (Romans 3:23). The only way sin is overcome in a human person is by God's grace (John 1:16-17, Romans 5:2, Ephesians 2:5-8). We cannot save ourselves – that is a principle tenet of the Word (Romans 6:14-15, Ephesians 2:5-10). Giving people the responsibility to undo severe mental or emotional disturbance, or to try and "fix" a situation that God may very well not be in is not in alignment with Biblical principles.

Modern Christian counseling eliminates any hope or goodness within the human person, believing it totally devoid of any goodness or hope without Christ. This is foundationally false. What the Word teaches us is that, because of sin, we cannot save ourselves (Ephesians 2:8-10, 1 Timothy 1:14). No matter how hard we try, our efforts to procure our own salvation are voided. As this theory about the total devoid nature of humanity is based in Calvinistic theory, we must begin to understand the human person beyond such belief.

I do not theorize people to be all good, or all bad. We are created in God's image (Genesis 1:26-27), and yet fallen, at the same time. This creates a paradox for the human being: our origins are with our Maker, our sinful, fleshly nature is with our enemy, and our redemption lies, once again, with our Maker. This full-circle approach to salvation lies in the "restoration" of all things, including human beings in the full image and likeness of God (Acts 3:21, 2 Peter 3:3-7). If the word "sin" is, as we have come to understand, missing the target, that means that we have hits and misses in our lives. To be a "sinner" does not mean every behavior, thought, or action of a person is, indeed sinful. We know from the Word that to be in violation of even one of God's precepts was to be a sinner (Acts 13:39, Romans 3:20, Galatians 5:3-4). Nobody completely misses everything, nor does everybody completely achieve everything. Right here we see people as more complex than just good or bad, noble or cowardly, or righteous or evil. By our nature, every one of is created in the image of God (Genesis 1:26-27). That basis for our creation does not change. Sin has changed the human condition, but it has not changed the fact that our original creation is in God's image. If God is good, that means that the blessings of God fall upon us as human beings. Intelligence, creativity, art, thought, science, writing, education, and other aspects of human life are, indeed, God-given. They are reflections of God's nature working within His people. Even though a person may miss God in their lives, they are not devoid of His presence or gifting within their lives. Sinfulness teaches us to scoff at what God has given, exploit it, or use it for ourselves. It teaches us to disregard God and one another. What sin cannot do, however, is make what God has given to us anything other than what He has given. Acknowledged or not, human beings still bear within them God's unique stamp of Himself. It doesn't make us God any more than sin makes us Satan himself. It simply means that human beings are more complicated than being all good or all bad by their very nature. This internal conflict is there, even within the sting of sin, to draw us unto God, that we may learn to find our completeness in Him.

The consequences of sin are also such that human beings are not simply sinners themselves; they also reap the results of sin in their lives. Hurting people need to recognize they cannot control other people, but by working with God, they can come to a place of accountability and responsibility over their own decisions and choices. Many of the wounds and hurts a person may experience in life are no fault of their own. Abuse, mistreatment and abandonment are not due to the results of the wounded person's sinfulness – they are the consequence of the sinful behaviors of others. No amount of personal behavioral correction is going to remove the hurts and wounds inflicted by others. If counseling is only about behavioral modification, this means it is not an agency of healing. Healing is beyond behavioral correction and beyond debates about sin – it is God's hand working in a person's life to transform and restore that which cannot be healed by human means.

Another severely missing component within Christian counseling is the total elimination of spiritual forces beyond the behavioral world. Christian counseling, by treating people as if they are programmable robots, fails to teach hurting people about the enemy they have. Denying Satan, demons, evil powers, witchcraft, possession, and the presence or force of evil in this world does a total disservice to understanding the issues behind those which we may face. While a situation may leave someone depressed, it's important we acknowledge that the force behind that situation may be evil, rather than just a negative state of human existence. People fall victim to any number of spiritual deceptions and issues that can also hamper or hurt their mental or spiritual well-being. Denying these issues is to deny the truth of spiritual realities.

It is obvious that the modern spin on that which is Christian and that which is counseling is a severe deviation from the healing agency of counseling. We will now explore the roots of this error – and how they are damaging believers worldwide.

The Christian subculture

In earlier times, Christians did not see their position in life as to withdraw from the world. Until the early twentieth century, Christians never saw a contradiction between science, medicine, history, and faith. The reason for this is simple: science, medicine, history, and faith were all largely intertwined. People explored God's creation and the world they lived in to see more of God at work and understand better the principles behind creation. Modern Christians, devoid of their history, often fail to realize Christians of years gone by (including the Founding Fathers of the United States) did not believe in God, in faith, and in Christianity as we do today; in fact, they would find the faith of today totally unrecognizable with the faith of their day. When Darwin's theory of evolution was first published, most Protestants accepted his theory, believing it to be a scientific account of creation. Prior to the Comstock Laws passed in the 1870s, one-third of all pregnancies ended in abortion, which was regarded as a form of birth control. It was not uncommon for women with women and men with men of certain status to live together in what was called a "Boston marriage." Most Christian leaders believed in paving the way, setting the all-important example when it came to current events and social causes. They were anything but uninvolved or isolated. While there were groups here and there that isolated themselves, most Christians believed their purpose was to be part of this world and represent the Gospel to the best of their understanding. Understandings came and went with various developments, life continued and changed, and Christians remained fixed in a position of change in the world.

The first major shift away from the world within Christianity was the advance of Fundamentalism. This was the first instance of an entire branch of Christianity establishing itself in direct contrast to a social belief or issue. In the past, divisions or conflicts within existing groups emerged over social issues (such as slavery, for example), but never entirely new denominational groups. The question is not so much as to what the Fundamentalists believed as the reason why the Fundamentalists did what they did. The Fundamentalists believed the secular world was evil and that Christianity needed to retreat from that world rather than stand to make change within it. This has been the growing trend of Christianity right down to the present day, with increasing hostility to concepts deemed to be of the "secular world." Each new step within this development has taken it to new heights: the Christian subculture now has its own clothing, branding, movies, music, imagery, educational systems, media, science, medicine, politics, social outlets, books, stores, products, marketing, and life applications. Rather than being about the Bible or remaining in the world, but not of it (John 16:33, John 17:11-18, 1 John 4:17), Christianity today is now marked by a lifestyle of isolation, completely unto itself, with no outreach or understanding of its purpose in the world whatsoever.

Becoming a Christian subculture creates an "us vs. them" mentality in the minds of unsuspecting believers, a common concept found within cult criteria. This same thinking is being perpetrated among Christians, only on a larger scale. To maintain the Christian subculture, certain figures within that movement must shape the way followers live, believe, and think. To do such, they make the rest of the world a source of distrust, inherent evil, and dangerous, with nothing to offer. This means that the average Christian equates Christian living with remaining separate, distant, and apart from anyone who does not think or believe as they do, thereby reducing the effectiveness of purpose and impact.

The reasons why Christian isolationism and subculture are dangerous are expansive and numerous, from leaving Christians vulnerable to predators, to the most simplistic reason of all: the relevance of the church in the world. It is God's will that Christians remain in the world to be relevant to the world – to provide salt and light in a lost and hurting world (Matthew 5:13-16). With modern sub-culture trends, the church is no longer forced to be current or in touch with the needs of this world. Christianity is withdrawing itself from the world to the point that it is of no relevance to the world's problems any longer. In a pursuit to separate from the world, the church has made anything that is not what it deems doctrinally Christian to be error.

To remain relevant to the world, we need to recognize that facts are God's truth in any situation and that truth does not begin and end with a current standard or substandard of its variance. There is no error between sound thinking and truth. Whether or not one has the entirety of God's Word is irrelevant to the fact that they may say something or receive knowledge of something from God, whether it is understood in its proper context or not. To deny what is true because it doesn't look like, sound like, or act like the current course of Christian thought is to deny the entirety of God's work in, with, and through humanity from the very beginning. Life, belief, and faith do not fit into neat, tidy little packages. The sooner we recognize this, the sooner we will be able to be relevant to the world again, not needing to isolate ourselves from it, but as part of it, without being what it is.

Christian materialism

Another severe error falls under the heading of the Christian subculture: Christian materialism. Throughout the ages, Christianity has had an uncomfortable and often contradictory relationship with materialism. History has displayed every conceivable principle possible, from required poverty for believers to lavish material wealth for the church, to lavish material wealth for its leaders at the expense of its people. The simplistic answer for the conflicts in materialism lie in a misunderstanding of God's precepts about the material world for the believer. God's Word does not make the material world of no value (Luke 6:38, 2 Corinthians 8:1-15), it simply puts materialism in a proper and balanced perspective. We can't become so materialistic that we ignore the Kingdom of God, nor can we become so spiritual that we forget about practical needs. God's Word provides for us the eternal balance, the ideal, by which we make the spiritual realm practical. From the beginning, God has always reached out to humanity with practical approach: through needs, hurts, solutions to problems, socialization, regulations, and perspectives. If we lose sight of this balance, we lose sight of God's use of His people to reach out to humanity.

The modern church has severely lost sight of this balance, erring now on the side of materialism versus the side of spirituality. The modern generation of churchgoers believes that God reaches out to humanity through material things in a concept commonly taught as prosperity (even though this errs from true understandings and teachings on prosperity as found in the Word). In this concept, people believe that God "rewards" them for faith with money or material things. As a result, it is believed that people who don't have enough or who are not financially or materially prosperous do not have enough faith, or the right faith. In this concept, as keeping with Christian subculture spoken of earlier, materialism is a defensive mechanism, a weapon, used to maintain social prestige or status – through faith.

If God's answer to humanity is to reach out through exclusively material ways, that makes God distant and spirituality void. It gives Him an ethereal, impractical quality because He can only be seen through a material possession – thereby indicating He cannot be seen or experienced through any other means than the material. It turns cars, houses, and money – things which anyone living in the material world can have – into miracles, whereby they are no such thing. It erases the need for the supernatural in our lives and creates believers that operate by a conditioned, Behaviorist response, to divinity. It also means they stop reaching out and continually pursue the material over the spiritual, thinking such will lead to a spiritual pursuit.

Disordered interpersonal relationships

The modern Christian media often talks about threats on the family and on family relationships. This is a clever tactic to continue Christian subculturalism and create that "us vs. them" mentality between the unsuspecting Christian and the world. By making the Christian believe that the world is out to get their family or destroy their family, Christians respond, in kind, by isolating their familial unit from the world. Something is hurting the Christian family, but it certainly is not the influence of the world. We would be mistaken to think the Christian family (and, by extension, the relationship of believers one to another in the church) has escaped the sting of the disordered thinking present in the Christian subculture.

Most Christian sub-cultural voices are, not surprisingly, male, and overwhelmingly patriarchal. Most of these voices, such as James Dobson (Focus on the Family), D. James Kennedy (deceased, but still largely influential), Pat Robertson (deceased, but fell out of vogue toward the end of his life), and Jerry Falwell (also deceased) could be described as having misogynistic tendencies. They advocate for the traditional view of patriarchy, with a husband as the head of his household and the women and children following closely behind in tow. We also see a high percentage of Christians believing in concepts of "covering" within the household, believing a woman to be eternally submissive to her husband, without proper understanding of Scripture's intentions in certain passages. These viewpoints are commonly held as "Christian values" without a single thought, when they are patriarchal viewpoints found in culture rather than in the Bible.

One of the biggest pitfalls of the Christian family today is this longing desire to bring back the values of another era when they feel the family was more relevant. The voices that be are quick to blame feminism, birth control, abortion, homosexuals, and any other assortment of things for what they deem to be the "breakdown" of family values. This cannot apply, however, if Christians have been a subculture for so many decades – thereby making the problems of Christianity their own. If we are to be honest, the concept of family has never had more relevance than it does now, and very much to the detriment of family dynamics and principles. Children are considered the most important "thing" to parents, and are expected to be spoiled, pampered, and the entire family life to revolve around them, while parents exhaust themselves to give the "best" to their children. The entirety of emotional needs, wants, and life revolves around children, who are undisciplined, poorly mannered, and self-centered. Too much responsibility is placed on the women in the relationship. Husbands and wives, trying too hard to meet with roles that God never mandated upon them, are at constant odds and never able to find fulfillment, not as a couple, and not as individuals. This over-emphasis on family is birthing an unsocialized family and, by extension, an unsocialized church.

Let's not pretend that Christian families do not experience dysfunction. Incidents of abuse, addiction, and disordered relationships are as prevalent in Christian denominations as they are within the world. Dysfunction exists because sin exists, and sin can rule a Christian family just as much as it can rule any other kind of family. What we must do in our relationships is seek God about the ways we can transform into His image and purpose for relationships. God has created us to be one to another, and we need to learn how we can better accomplish that instead of delegating out roles designed in patriarchal error.

Disordered church identity and authority

In keeping with views of patriarchy, the modern church has distorted God's precepts for church authority and God's established church structure, which is the five-fold ministry structure of apostles, prophets, evangelists, pastors, and teachers found in Ephesians chapter 4. In conjunction with distorting leadership, we now also face a distorted understanding of the church and the church's purpose in the world.

If we consider the current concept of local churches and pastors, they exactly conform to patriarchal concepts of the family: the pastor is the head of that local church, not extending beyond those boundaries of influence, and in that exclusivity, the pastor is the chief authority, a father-figure, to that local church. Within that local sphere of influence, nobody is higher, nor has more say or purpose, than that pastor. The current image we have of a pastor very eerily reflects American values, rather than Biblical ones, and American images, rather than spiritual ones.

Not only is this not the Biblically stipulated office for the pastor, it also leaves the pastor isolated and disconnected. The result of the leadership's isolation (characterized by aggrandizing pastoral control and sphere of influence) carries over into our entire view and system of church and ministry. If the church is a local entity, that means it is not a universal one. Losing sight of the universal church (by abolishing the offices of apostle, prophet, and evangelist) causes the church to look inward upon itself, rather than seeking to reach out to the world.

Pastors need direction, training, and correctional checking – not a free hand. Patriarchal notions of "head of household" do not have a place within God's ministry order. That is not in accordance with God's purpose for the pastor, which is to be a shepherd. Without the universal church, the pastor doesn't have a sense of his or her position as a local authority. Without the rest of the five-fold, the pastor cannot rightly do his or her job and stand in that office with understanding and conviction. Pastors without a right vision and sense get lost and often stray into doctrinal untruth or control issues, which, without apostles, prophets, and evangelists, go unchecked.

This raises the point that the purpose of the church has been lost in our modern understanding therein. Most people understand the church to be a building, limited by local space and authority, in various places throughout the world. This modern concept alienates the church from its true purpose. The church is the body of Christ. The purpose of the church is to be the Kingdom of God here on earth. If local communities come out of the Kingdom work of the church, that's purposed and wonderful. Too much emphasis is made on the local communities today, and that has led to too many churches, too many conflicts in leadership, too much competition, and not enough work for the Kingdom. If our job is to be the Body of Christ, that means the church local must be connected to the worldwide work of the Body. This is accomplished through the universal offices of apostle, prophet, and evangelist – as these three offices bridge the universal church with the local church. Local churches need to realize they are a part of the universal church, not the other way around. Understanding the purpose of the church – to make the presence of Jesus Christ and His saving work known in the world – is a universal call that takes everyone. Patriarchy and local isolation have no place in the true church of Jesus Christ.

The loss of purpose

The last issue that we are going to look at is the loss of purpose, both within the individual and the church, which causes people to seek what they are lacking in any number of places.

The concept of a subculture indicates a fixed set culture within a culture. It is, in terms of demographics, considered a part of larger culture, but is its own entity, unto itself, within the larger culture. Christianity today meets the definition of a subculture, as was discussed earlier, because it exists as part of a larger culture. This inward pull continues onward into the self, rather than extending out. Whereas Christian subculture was once noted by a denomination or a body of denominations, the Christian subculture then became noted by local areas, and then even smaller by the local church. Nowadays, the Christian subculture, while drawing to local churches, is largely dependent upon the individual and the immediate extensions of the individual, such as family.

The materialism, isolation, and exclusivist present in modern Christianity has created an individualistic mindset, where faith, belief, and understanding are all about the individual. Instead of becoming a part of a bigger body, the relationship with God becomes all about that person's perspective of God and what God can do for him or her. This draws people inward, on an exclusive and personal understanding of God where there is no hope for growth or maturity. In the process, a person loses sight of purpose: everything is about them, all the time. They are isolated into a world of nothingness where the total focus is on getting needs met, their problems getting fixed, and totally forget about the bigger issues at hand, present in both the church and the world.

We only find purpose when we are connected to the Body of Christ. If people are isolated unto themselves, they cannot find purpose. A lack of purpose leads to problems in faith and problems in life. It's not an accident that so many disturbances exist and so much guidance is needed in today's church. As the church has lost its purpose – to reach humanity with the Gospel as the Kingdom of God – it is not an accident that the believers have too faltered in purpose and do not understand their place or position within God's Kingdom and the world at large.

The solution for Christian counseling

It's evident that the problems present in Christian counseling are only a byproduct of many issues present in the church as a whole. Many would say there is no answer to the issues, and that they cannot be helped. I disagree. Since this text is on Christian counseling, that is what we are going to examine – and how Christian counseling can be fixed to become the healing agency God designed it to be.

Christian counseling needs to be redesigned, from the ground up. In this text, this is how we will do just that:

- Christian counseling needs to be more than a theoretical approach to issues – it needs to pose practical answers to emotional, spiritual, and life issues. It needs to make spirituality tangible, rather than ethereal. Instead of saying, "God will solve your problems," it needs to be the practical answer to HOW God will solve your problems.

- As Christian counselors, we must redefine our approach to the human being and incorporate a holistic approach to patient care. People are not just a disorder, a problem, or a sin – they are people, and need to be treated as such.

- We need to draw on the types and shadows present in the history of psychoanalytical theory and see how God educates us about the human mind and person as contained therein. We need to balance mental analysis and different theories with the Bible, instead of assuming them to be contradictory.

- We need to stop assuming everything that quotes a Bible verse or a Bible teaching is Biblical. Just because something claims to be

Biblical or about the Bible – maybe even quote a few references – doesn't mean that it is indeed Biblical. This is especially relevant in Christian counseling.

- The Christian counselor needs to assume the roles of balance in his or her own life. In a true atmosphere of Christian counseling, the counselor has the challenge of balancing three areas of truth: the spiritual, the practical, and the emotional. This incorporates elements of personal responsibility, modification where applicable, and training in appropriate spiritual warfare as pertains to counseling issues. Where a Christian counselor is unqualified, they must have the professionalism to step aside for someone who is qualified.

- The church needs to restore counseling as a practice, beyond counseling at the altar or altar calls, and restore the dignity of the prophetic work and nature in counseling.

Chapter Review

<u>Essay Questions</u>

Construct a well-written essay (minimum 5-8 sentences), answering the following question.

- Based on the text, your own thoughts and own opinions, what do you think about the current state of Christianity? What do you believe are some things that are hurting the church today? How can Christian counseling help heal some of the issues present today?

SECTION II

Redefining Christian
Counseling

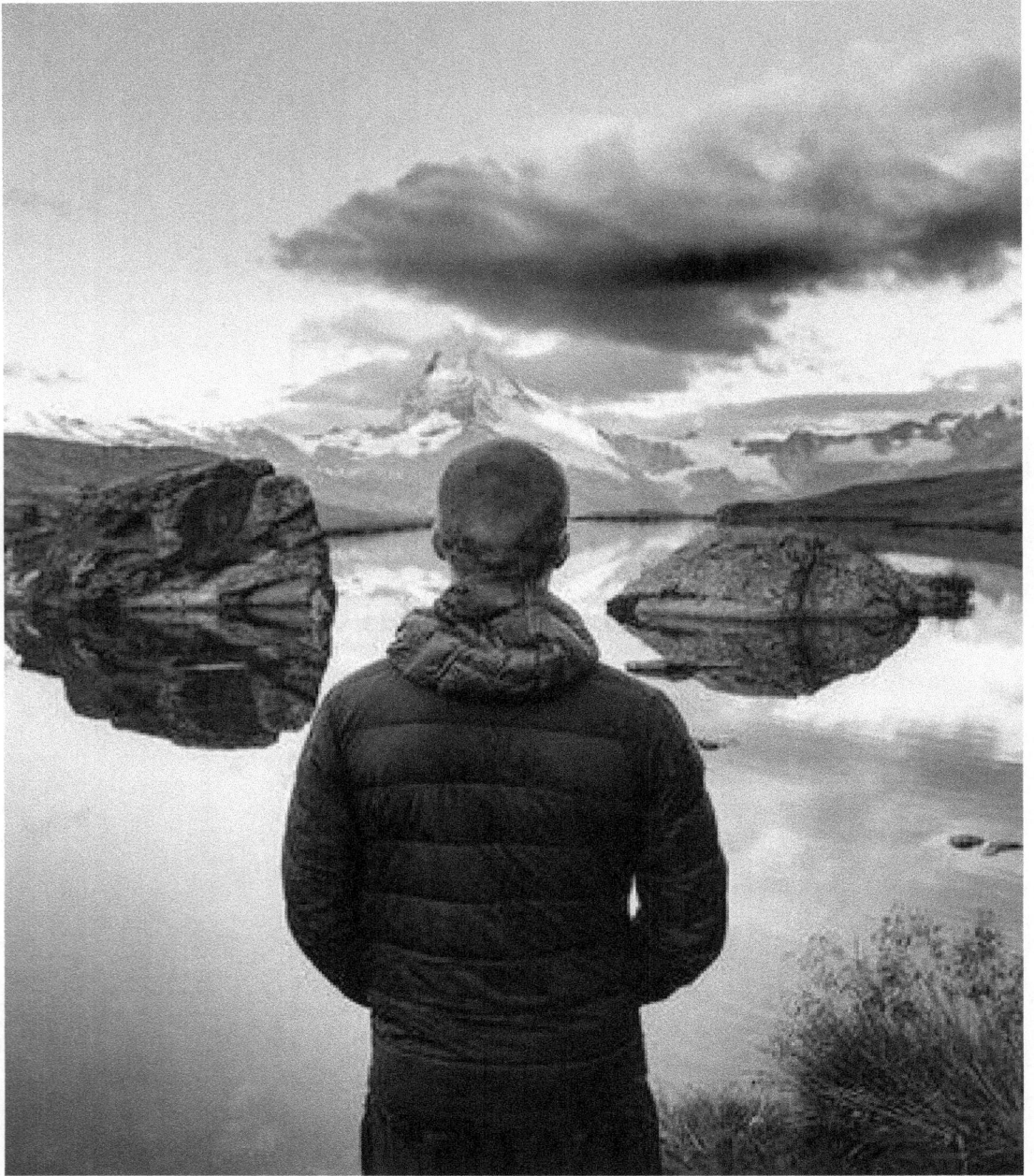

CHAPTER ELEVEN

Types and Shadows in Traditional Psychoanalytical Theory

Who has put wisdom in the innermost being?
Or given understanding to the mind?
- Job 38:36

The current trends in Christian counseling serve to denounce traditional psychoanalytical theory, believing it is ungodly. From years of study and research, there are many reasons why this approach is both unbiblical and impractical.

Psychoanalysis and psychoanalytical research have delved into areas of science that, whether we like to admit it or not, religion has not sought to investigate. In the world of spirituality and religion, the traditional stance has been to remain the same, remain consistent, and to follow a course of what seems right or continual from the beginning. This type of attitude and mentality has served to keep the church in a stagnant place.

In this chapter, we are going to look again – in brief – at the different psychoanalysts mentioned in the last section of this book and how we can draw themes useful for Christian counseling from them. To understand what we are going to do, we must first understand God's principle of working by "types and shadows."

Types and shadows

God's principle of types and shadows is simple: it is when God uses one thing as a type, or illustration, of something else. The term "type" and "shadow" are used interchangeably: just as a shadow reflects someone or something else, but is not the person itself, so a spiritual shadow does the same thing. The type or shadow of something points to something else. It is not, within itself, the reality within itself, but points to a greater reality.

Christian theologians and apologists have spent many years illustrating types and shadows of Christ as present within the Old Testament and then revealed in the New Testament. What many of them fail to see is typology beyond the person and prophecy of Jesus Christ. Everything in the New Testament is shadowed in the Old Testament, from the largest detail to the smallest ones. Offices, people, places, teachings, and most importantly, the Kingdom of God, are all in the Old Testament, right along with Christ, waiting for their day and prophetic unveiling. We recognize the Passover lamb and the water from the rock as types of Christ (Exodus 12:21, Exodus 17:1-6), but often forget Israel also typifies the Kingdom of God (Psalm 7:7, Psalm 22:22-25, Psalm 89:5). Many of the prophets of old connect to powerful New Testament figures as types of the five-fold ministry offices (Moses, Deborah, Elijah, and Malachi, to name a few).

Typology is the way God shadows Himself upon the world. It is the way He reveals Himself to us: in bits and pieces, here and there, that we will find Him in our common, everyday existence. This is how spirituality transcends the distant and moves into the practical. It makes the message of salvation visible in the most unexpected places, seeing creation as subject to God, and the world and all contained therein as part of His eternal plan. The most essential mistake many Christians make is thinking the system of types and shadows has ended. It has ended in terms of typifying the coming of the Messiah, but God is still moving within His people and revealing Himself to humanity, that humanity may receive Him. We can also see God moving in various types and shadows to reach us in a deeper way, piece by piece, as we come to see Him in a fuller way. We know that this side of heaven we see through a glass darkly (1

Corinthians 13:12), and typology is that way by which we come to know God more and more as He shows Himself to us, everywhere.

Typology present among non-believers

One of the most undeveloped areas of typology is typology beyond the Bible, delving into typology in the world, or the typology present within creation. As God uses what is earthly to teach us about Him, typology is always used through God's creation, those things found on earth: created things or created people to teach on deeper spiritual things. Many theologians have not thought about typology deep enough to delve into this area of belief beyond the Scriptures.

To understand typology among non-believers (and even see typology among believers in a deeper sense), we need to move beyond literalism. We can literally hold to certain ideas or concepts, or we can start to see God reaching out to humanity in ways beyond our literalism. If we choose to do this, we will see God moving in people's lives and it will help us to understand His dealings with humanity, rather than limiting it to His work within and through us.

Romans chapter 1 has been debated for centuries. It is often invoked to aggravate certain political conditions, but it's important we don't see it as a weapon. Most of the Bible was about God's dealings with the people He called His own, who agreed to meet His conditions, and the struggles therein to meet God's will throughout the ages. We must not make the mistake of thinking, however, that God has not reached out to the non-believer. The numerous examples in God's Word of His dealings with Gentiles (such as Ruth, Rahab, and Vashti) show us that God has been working to reach the entire world with His truth since the beginning of time. Romans 1 is about this difference: it is about typology among those who were non-believers.

Romans 1 outlines the practical truth that even the pagan, and the Gentile at large (a word that means "nations") had knowledge of God. If we study the history of pagan or neo-pagan religion, we can see they had a distinct understanding of the laws and workings of nature. Pagan cycles are based entirely around agricultural cycles: sowing and reaping, seedtime and harvest, cold and hot, the sun, moon and stars, and winter, spring, summer, and fall. Through their intimate knowledge with creation and creation's elements, the pagans had knowledge of God and God's "types." As God works His types through the ordinary, the pagan had knowledge of God's laws and God's principles through His "types" present in creation. Romans 1 goes on to clarify the error of the pagan peoples: instead of turning toward their Creator, they turned toward creation and idolized it. So, in other words, they were the ones at fault: it wasn't that the type was not present, not recognized, or that God had not reached out to them, it was simply that they idolized the type.

What this teaches us is that everything that may not bear God's full truth does contain a type of truth therein. In everything, God is reaching out to humanity, through thoughts, wisdom, the insights of human beings, His creation, and the ordinary experiences by which He reveals Himself to us, so that we might find Him. It is true that people continue to make the mistake of the ancients by worshipping the type rather than the One Who put that type in place, but it does not mean that the type is not there, waiting to be revealed.

The application of typology in a proper understanding doesn't mean that everything leads to salvation, is perfect, or is holy. It's obvious that the water from the rock, while it was a type of Christ, did not cause anyone to be saved. If people stopped and started worshipping the rock, thereby taking it out of its context, it would have held no power as such – but would not have ceased being a type. It, in and of itself, held no power – but what it pointed to did hold power. Typology, properly applied, does not mean that all paths lead to God; but it does mean that God is teaching us through everything and can teach us through anyone who seeks insight into His creation. The principle of typology is clear in that it is pointing us to something greater through things both brilliant and extraordinary. It is God working through that which acknowledges Him as much as working through that which does not acknowledge Him. Behind all things, typology proves that God is in control, whether acknowledged or not.

Types and shadows applied to Christian counseling

As Christian counselors, we need to see the relevance of typology in the application of our research and study into the human mind. In the case of Christian counseling, that means that God teaches us through types and shadows of His revelation through traditional psychoanalytical theory. This does not mean the people who brought forth the shadows of truth were adherents of the faith we hold true, nor does it recognize that everything they said we should adhere to as Gospel. What it does mean is we need to recognize the wisdom, understanding, and God's wisdom made applicable to us through the theories and methods of traditional psychoanalysts.

The unsanctified mind

Traditional psychoanalytical theory was devoted to those who were mentally ill or severely mentally disturbed; it was not for those who were mentally well and balanced. If we look closely at traditional theory, it gives us great insight into the mind that has not yet put on the mind of Christ (1 Corinthians 2:16, 2 Corinthians 3:14) or remains with any trace that has not been transformed by Christ. Taking Freudian theory, for example, the man or woman who operates solely by impulse and drive has not put on the mind of Christ, with the evidence of the fruit of self-control (1 Corinthians 9:25, Galatians 5:23). Switching back and forth between behaviors is a sign of instability, of being Biblically "double minded." If we do not walk by the Holy Spirit, we will behave irrationally and not understand the force driving us to behave as we do. Someone dealing with repression, and living in a state of denial, cannot live in victory and receive the mind of Christ because they are too cluttered and will behave defensively in response. The ultimate goal, however, of the unsanctified mind is to find liberation, freedom, from bondage. Even Freudian theory recognizes there is a process for liberation, a redemption, for the unsettled, unsanctified mind. Such realizes that going to accept an altar call is not enough for a person to transform by the mind of Christ: it is a process by which we are transformed into His image.

Moving on to the Jungian process, Jungian theory delved into a different aspect of the unsanctified mind. He recognized the relevance of spiritual development in the process of mental health and stability. Whatever spirituality he practiced as a person is not specific to the injunction that we should practice the same; Jung was simply advocating people connect on a spiritual level with God. Recognizing the spiritual in our lives awakens us to our reality and helps us to delve into something deeper. This message is the same one we give to anyone who does not yet know God, it is just specialized on the issues and theories of the mind that does not know God. Jungian theory proves that spirituality in someone's life can make a difference. Now, many years after Jung first purported his theory, there is evidence to its truth.

Adler's theories about inferiority also echo the truth of the unsanctified mind. Aggression, much like sex, is not evil in and of itself, but can become destructive when applied to sinful actions. We know that without God, we can do nothing to save or help ourselves. We cannot have a proper sense of ourselves if we do not have God in our lives. Transforming ourselves to the mind of Christ also connects us to the Body of Christ, part of Adlerian belief as relates to environment or community. God has created us to be one to another, and the way we interact one to another affects all of us. Until we are in Christ in a true and lasting sense, we will deal with issues pertaining to inferiority and superiority. People are more than their problems, and Adler reminds us of this. In our case, people are more than just a sinful state. They are created in the image of God and yes, they have issues and problems, but God can transform people from sinners to saints.

Horney's theories too help us to see the unsanctified mind at work. People who encounter problems and do not have the tools to overcome are going to continue to encounter those issues throughout life. It cannot be healed if it is not confronted and peace restored. If we are struggling with constant issues, we will respond in specific ways to people, much like Karen Horney described: with clinginess, power and control struggles, or excessive autonomy.

The possessed mind

Traditional psychoanalytical theory also gives us stark insight into the mind of someone who is possessed. The Bible, while speaking of demonic possession, tends to reflect the level of current medical understanding reflecting the time in which it was written. The focus in those days was on the physical ailment and the physical manifestation of such, and therefore, did not focus on the mental manifestation of such an ailment. Freud, Jung, Horney, Klein, and Adler all bring to light the mental state of patients struggling with neurosis and mental illness – the way they function, their patterns of reasoning and thought, and often, even ways possession may have entered their lives (such as through trauma or abuse). Their methods are innovative for handling such as we realize they did not advocate patients to be restrained in beds, beaten or whipped, or placed in hot baths to "steam out demons." They advocated humane treatment, and counteractions to demonic behaviors as having more than one approach.

Essential stages of development in the human person

All psychoanalysts studied certain aspects about human development and normal human development within a person. Freud, in particular, was explicitly clear about various stages of development essential for the development of the healthy and balanced human person. Recognizing his various stages helps us to see the process of socialization, by which human beings are acclimated to being part of their larger society and world. Part of our measure of well-being comes from the behaviors we exhibit to other human beings. God has created us fearfully and wonderfully and marking the different stages of human behavior gives us a greater appreciation for normalcy in God's plan for our development.

God requires His people to be socialized. Many of the Old Testament regulations surrounding hygiene, business, interactions with one another, relatives, foreign neighbors, and even interactions with animals all related to socialization. God was teaching His people how to become and interact as a socialized people. The normal stages of human development help to set us on the course of socialization throughout life, able to work, live, interact, and yes, even worship with one another.

The principles of life and death at work in the universe

The basic principles of life (*eros*, the libido) and death (*thanos*) are very essential to the theories of Freud, Adler, and Horney. They recognized there are driving forces, that which strives for life, and those which center on entropy and push toward death. We know the Word teaches us on the polarity of life and death (Proverbs 12:28, Proverbs 18:21, Jeremiah 21:8) and on the choice to pursue life over death (Deuteronomy 30:15-19, John 5:24). If we are not pursuing life, our lives will be filled with death. If we are pursuing life, we can overcome death. The pursuit of psychotherapy and Christian counseling, at large, is to overcome death principles and help people to live.

A whole-person approach

The essence of holism is that people are more than a problem or disorder they may have: they are human beings, and many components make up humanity. Within the precept of holism is also its counter response: the temptation to completely identify someone due to a disorder or issue. Horney, Maslow and Adler believed this was relevant to the success of patient care. As Christian counselors, we too should recognize the relevance in treating people as a whole rather than just a part. We can understand that Jesus came to heal people everywhere they hurt – not just perhaps in areas of personal sin or wrongdoing – and that Jesus never identified people as their sins. People are sinners, but they are not their sins – nor are they their disabilities or ailments. While we may be treating someone for something specific, we cannot lose sight of that person as created in the image of God and created with purpose, despite their situation.

The complexity of the human being

While all theories of psychoanalysis delve into complex areas of human behavior and human existence, Jungian theory in particular expounds the complex nature of human behavior, interaction, personality, desire, and interest. In contrast to theories such as B.F. Skinner's, Jungian theory and the theories of many other psychotherapists prove the complexity of our make-up. We know from Scriptural understanding that people are spiritual as well as physical, intellectual as well as conditioned, and that we have every ability to resist things in our lives or to react to things within our lives. People have thoughts, feelings, opinions, beliefs, convictions, and dispositions that all come together to create the wonderful fabric of human existence. The way one person may perceive something may not be the way someone else perceives it. If we try to reduce human beings to a simple concept of conditioning or early-birth environment, we will fail to see the beauty in God's creation present in the human being. It is essential that Christian counselors take full consideration of the complexity of people into their counseling, and do not reduce people to any one thing or situation.

Types and shadows of spiritual development

Jungian theory is also a powerful type for shadows of spiritual development. Just as Freud discussed the different stages of physical development, Jung provides us insight into different aspects of spiritual development through the process of individualization. The first stage of spiritual development could be considered the "awakening" of the psyche, as Jung spoke of. As believers, we know the first stage to our walk with God was to be awakened to ourselves – aware of who we are and our state of being – and our state of sinfulness and our need of God – and often, along with that, awakened to our purpose. We then progress through different stages of spiritual development: becoming an individual, discovering our identity in Christ, developing an understanding of walking in the flow of the Spirit and receiving power from the Spirit; and that God may speak to us using various images and symbols we have retained from early on in our lives.

The relevance of dreams

Freud and Jung believed in the importance of dream analysis because they believed that dreams held keys to understanding the desires, wishes, and concepts of their patients. To many, a dream state represents a bridge between consciousness and unconsciousness. As Christians, we should never write off the dreams people have as useless or irrelevant. We know the Word teaches on the power of the prophetic, and that God reveals much to us through our dreams. What we often fail to consider in dreams that don't seem as obvious about prophetic people or situations is that God may also be revealing things to us about ourselves. Don't assume a dream is irrelevant; examine it and take it in prayer. If you do not have a gift to interpret dreams, suggest they see someone who can.

Beginnings matter

All psychoanalysts: Freud, Jung, Horney, Klein, Adler, Maslow, Skinner and Fromm believed in the essence of good beginnings. While they did not all agree on the same way to get to good beginnings or to overcome bad beginnings, they all believed that where we start out in life matters. While it is possible to overcome bad beginnings, it's also important not to overlook things that may have happened earlier in someone's life. As with all things, balance is very important. Using bad beginnings as an excuse to remain stuck or remain in a bad place is just as bad as ignoring the relevance of roots in a problem. It's also important we look beyond beginnings as a simple aspect of childhood living. The foundations to our faith, to our calling in Christ, to the work we do in our lives, to our relationships with others, to our current lives as adults are all relevant beginnings to examine in the course of counseling.

Words bear power

Free association, founded by Freud and a cornerstone to all psychoanalytical theory, operates on the principle that as people speak of different experiences and issues they may have, they are able to bring their repressed issues to the surface. This bears the spiritual principle that what we say holds power over us and that by our words we can set ourselves free or we can remain in bondage.

The basics of human needs

Today people believe there are a myriad of things essential for human life, from technology, to free access to birth control, to certain types of cuisine or housing. It is easy for people to feel deprived because they don't have what someone else has or feel inferior to others for any number of reasons. We also encounter the danger of indignance, the deeper these concepts divide. Maslow, Fromm, and Horney all examined the basis for both practical and emotional needs in human beings. If we see someone without something, such as food or clothing, that is a need that must be met before emotional needs can be met. Needs are practical, not extravagant, in life. Helping people to gain perspective on need vs. want and priority vs. hopes and wishes is an essential part to balanced counseling that sees people through to a better life.

The dangers of religion as projection of wish fulfillment

Freud was notably against organized religion, because he believed its theologies and perspectives were the projections of things people wished for in their lives, but either didn't have or desired to have. He felt that such pursuits encouraged denial and delusion in people. Even though Freud's theory downplayed theology in general, I think that he raised a certain point we need to be aware of, especially in counseling. Many people project God in their own image, rather than conforming themselves to His image. It is not uncommon to find people who have a concept of God that is akin to a Santa Claus or a doting parent, who simply exists for their own purposes and never corrects or disciplines them. It is very dangerous to live with such a concept of God, because this means they do not see God as the ultimate authority figure, and do not understand that they need to live and walk in obedience to Him.

As counselors, we also need to deter ourselves from transmitting this kind of concept onto our patients. It is not uncommon to find counselors who operate more as motivational speakers on a one-on-one level. Brushing people off with trite sayings, dispensing advice without proper information, and acting like a cheerleader instead of a counselor creates a situation where the client cannot trust you. It is equally important to avoid telling patients that God will do something specific in a situation without any divine guidance or using clichés ("God's got a great plan for your life!") without truly listening and empathizing to your patient. Do not give the impression that God just dumps finances and answers on people and magically solves problems with the snap of a finger.

While Fromm did not teach against religion in the way Freud did,

Fromm's perspectives also tap into the same type of danger. If faith remains archaic, it does not help people to solve their issues in our modern times. Sometimes we must look upon the words of Scripture and allow them to come to life or apply in a different way than maybe we grew up having or grew up understanding. If God's Word is alive and active, we must constantly go to the Word and see new ways we can understand and apply it to have it apply for us in our day and for the things we are going through.

Instead of using faith as an excuse to remain in denial or not deal with issues, make faith a practical part of a client's healing process. Work to make the presence of God known in a difficult situation and God standing with that person to heal and walk them through their healing process — not pretend the issue at hand is nonexistent. Use practical concepts as found in the Word to encourage people to continue to walk out difficulties, not run away from them. Allow the Word to be practical, rather than unobtainable.

Being a "good person" is not enough

Most of society believes that being a "good person" is enough to get people both through this life and into heaven. We know from the Word that it is not sufficient for salvation, but if we closely examine the Word, we learn it is also not sufficient to get us through this life. Maslow's entire theory, present in both his hierarchy of needs and other beliefs included in his theory, proves that we need to be more than just "good people:" we need to be people who seek and excel in purpose. Jesus told us that He did not just come so we would have life, but would have abundant life (John 10:10). It is not God's will for us to live without discovering our full purpose and His full promise to us in this life, which is what psychoanalytical theory defines as being "self-actualized." God's promises to us don't just get us better in touch with God; they also get us better in touch with ourselves, and the work we are to do to better mankind. As Christian counselors, we work to help motivate people unto purpose by helping them heal from issues in their lives.

Men, women, and non-binary are not the same

Christian counselors often use the differences in the sexes against women and in favor of men. They continue to perpetrate the issues of society upon women and use counseling to psychologically intimidate or pervade against women in favor of patriarchal perspectives. The truth is that there are differences between men and women, and the Word of God does point this out. Men and women have different viewpoints, understandings of life, and perspectives on many issues. On the other hand, the desires and drives of men and women are not as different as we would like to think, and God's Word proves this as well. The difference between men and women is often in the approach to these drives, and the encounters and concepts to heal may also be different.

Modern psychology has deviated deeply from foundational positions about men and women, so much so that it is almost universally accepted that men and women cannot understand each other. If we look at earlier psychoanalytical theory, there doesn't seem to be such an intense and severed rift between understanding of the sexes. Even though it may not have been their intention, earlier psychoanalytical theory served to reconcile more of a Biblical harmony between the sexes than modern theories. Freud and Horney both spoke of envies between the two, and quite honestly, at that. Consequences of sin include power and control struggles between men and women, and such leads to both penis envy and womb envy as the two strive for control over the other. This basic reality must be admitted and acknowledged before we can strive for understanding and unity between the two.

The work of both Adler and especially Horney reminds us that women are not the same as men, and that society does not treat women the same way it treats men. The different way society treats men and women is based in an automatic inequality on the part of women that affects the way she may perceive herself, her position in life, and her pursuits throughout her life. Women need to be treated differently in counseling and encouraged to discover themselves as entities separate and distinct from men and their families. It is even more important that a woman comes to a place of self-discovery and of calling in Christ because of these different issues present in society. Healing is essential in women, because society encourages women in both repression and over-emotionalism, which can cause many issues, including instability. It is also important that men are encouraged to change their perspectives on women through counseling, valuing them as people with thoughts, desires, purpose, and ideas. When both men and women are valued for their purposes in this world, both can better discover God's purpose and great unity between the two for Kingdom development. For a sense of overall self-esteem, both sexes need to accomplish things for themselves outside of other beings and outside of marriage, children, and family.

Beyond the questions of natural biology, we also find the issue that non-binary and transgender needs also vary from that of men and women. Recognizing the specific needs – with central identity, as is true for all beings, as child of God – makes a huge difference in laying a proper foundation for spiritual understanding. When a non-binary or transgender individual knows their inherent worth and value, it sets them on a course to discover things such as purpose, self-esteem, and fulfillment of divine destiny.

<u>Children and adults are not the same</u>

Thousands of years ago, the Bible acknowledged the simple fact that children and adults are different. They do not interact in the same way as adults, and do not have the same needs. We know this is true because the Bible encourages adults to train up children in the right way to go (Proverbs 22:6). This clearly indicates to us that the way children are handled in counseling is different than the way adults are handled. Klein's approach using play therapy shows that children need counseling techniques on their own level, and play is a perfect way to do that.

<u>Correcting behavior</u>

B.F. Skinner's theories were extreme, but he does point out the relevance of behavioral correction. While behavior is not completely dictated by conditioning, it is important not to underestimate the value in behavioral correction. The Bible's entire purpose is a lesson in behavior correction, correcting the ways of sin via consequence and blessing obedience via reward. When we encounter someone in counseling with a behavioral issue, it is important not to encourage such behavior but point out the span of consequence accompanied by such behavior and the result of consequences from actions. In many circumstances, changing behavior comes about as a result of discovery, and behavioral change can never be ignored in the process of Christian counseling.

The importance of love and being loved

Central to Fromm's theory was a belief in the practicality of love and its purpose beyond just an emotion or feeling designed to help people mate. The Word of God has taught this principle for well over 2,000 years! The love we have must be tangible to be life changing. It is such a deep despair to see people who have never experienced or felt love in a tangible way and to encounter people who do not understand how to make love tangible. Those in need of healing and hope need to experience the love of God through God's people, and especially through God's counselor. When love becomes practical, it becomes transforming.

The power of freedom

All psychoanalytical theories seek to help people discover freedom from various mental ailments. Fromm expands the relevance of freedom into the realm of both society and social interaction. The Word of God talks about the essence of freedom from sin (Romans 8:21, Galatians 5:1), but it also teaches us about freedom in victory (Isaiah 61:1, 2 Peter 2:19). Overcoming the various issues that cause us to be bound are essential for healing and victory within Christian counseling. Jesus' power to free does not only apply to sin, but to every type of ailment that affects us in this life.

We are not ever going to figure out certain parts of human personality, persona, being, or other people

Jung believed there were things we could not ever know about the unconscious mind, simply because it is unconscious. This is a true shadow and reality about both the human mind and about other people. No matter how much we study, inquire, or delve into human issues, problems, and thoughts, there are forever going to be issues that remain only a type or shadow for us as we view things this side of heaven. Sometimes problems are never fully revealed to us, nor appear to be fully resolved, because as long as we live in the world, we will battle "thorns in the flesh." This does not make counseling a failure – it simply makes it a divine tool and spiritual gift we use this side of heaven to help humanity along as we go through this life.

Chapter Review

<u>Essay Questions</u>

Construct a well-written essay (minimum 5-8 sentences), answering the following question.

- Explain, in detail, the principle of types and shadows and way types and shadows apply to Christian counseling today.

CHAPTER TWELVE

Ethics in Christian Counseling

Therefore, since we have this ministry, as we received mercy, we do not lose heart, but we have renounced
the things hidden because of shame, not walking in craftiness or adulterating the Word of God,
but by the manifestation of truth commending ourselves to every man's conscience in the sight of God.
And even if our gospel is veiled, it is veiled to those who are perishing, in whose case the god of this world
has blinded the minds of the unbelieving so that they might not see the light of the gospel of the glory of Christ,
Who is the image of God.
- 2 Corinthians 4:1-4

Another primary issue within Christian counseling is the issue of ethics. With the advance of modern ministers who operate ministry work without training and qualifications, ethics are a major issue in the modern counseling scene. From gossip about a counselor's patient under the guise of "prayer" to confusion about who may be present during a counseling session, a lack of professional ethics has become a landmine of lawsuits, damaged reputations, and problems for Christian counselors. If we are to revitalize, change, and empower the walk of the Christian counselor, we need to understand the essential role ethics play in Christian counseling.

What are ethics?

Ethics are standards of honesty, broken down and assessed by situations and circumstances, for every aspect of an individual's dealings with other human beings in an interactive sense. In other words, ethics are principles by which we live and interact with individuals when dealing in business, ministry, and other professional settings. Ethics are professional standards of honesty and integrity.

Because "ethics" is a term often used by business professionals in the world, many Christians believe ethics are not a part of Christian professionalism. Many within today's church like to think that the church operates by its own set of guidelines, or many times, lack thereof. The concepts of business, professionalism, and ethics often fall by the wayside as people prefer to see the church in a family setting, where everything is told to everyone else.

Just as in keeping with the "family" concept, not all information is available to everyone else. Some things remain between a husband and a wife, some things between parents and children, some things between siblings, and some things remain within a household. The same is applicable within the church: some information is just not for public consumption. That is when the role of counselor and patient comes into play. It is also worth noting that certain standards of professionalism and ethics are just a part of counseling, whether we are Christian counselors or secular counselors. Christian counselors must abide by ethics to operate effectively in this ministerial work and empowerment.

There are certain basic foundational ethics involved in counseling. In this chapter, we will examine these different ethical precepts. If a counselor is found to be in violation of such, they open themselves up to lawsuits, disagreeable reputation, and revocation of their counselor's or minister's license.

Confidentiality

The principal foundation of any counseling session and any counselor-client relationship is confidentiality. Confidentiality means that the details of sessions are not for public revelation in direct relation to the details given. To explain this principle: the details of counseling sessions are not to be revealed by association to other people, unless there is a circumstance by which a counselor believes a person to be in danger.

Counselors must maintain a certain balance when dealing with patients. This means that they cannot be easily shocked or unsettled by revealed details. As part of the counseling process, certain things will be said that may be shocking to the sensibilities of the counselor. It is most difficult in this state to handle confidentiality, due to the shock factor. It is also difficult to maintain confidentiality when we have been told something we feel others should know about. The bottom line of a confidentiality guarantee is that it remains confidential, including notes, recorded records, and files on patients.

In terms of Christians, the major threats to confidentiality are gossip and giving too much information to prayer lines or friends. Confidentiality is an essential seal of trust and an important bond between a counselor and their client. Clients aren't friends you can gossip about over lunch, nor are they people who you can just speak freely about at any time. In terms of the ethics gap, clients must be handled professionally and with dignity. These people are confiding in someone with the ability and professionalism to help them, not tell other people. Violating confidentiality violates trust.

When relating to counseling experiences (such as in teaching, training, or writing for case studies) or requesting prayer for patients, details must be kept to a minimum. Patients should not be exposed via prayer requests. A simple "I have a client who is battling various spiritual, physical, and emotional issues. Please keep them in prayer" is sufficient. We do not need to tell everyone every detail to request prayer. A good method to use when requesting prayer, as well, is to request that all those you counsel are remembered in prayer, without having to name names or give excessive information.

Counselors likewise must refrain from approaching clients in public, only responding if a client speaks to them directly. Matters of session should not be discussed in public under any circumstances.

When counseling is done as part of a "word" on the altar, it must be handled with confidentiality, as well. People's business does not need to be aired out to an entire group of people. Remove the microphone and speak directly and quietly to them. If someone requires more extensive counseling, have people available to assist with this matter privately during the service. We will discuss this issue a little more in detail in a later chapter.

The major exception made in instances of confidentiality pertains to professional guidance. Sessions may be discussed with superiors or colleagues. If a counselor has a question in regard to how to handle a patient and the superior works as part of the firm, they do have access to patient information. Colleagues, however, are another matter entirely. It is essential that names are not mentioned, and details are kept to a general minimum.

Who can be present for sessions?

In keeping with confidentiality, those who are present for a session need to be those who are relevant to that session. That means if it is a personal counseling session, the only people who should be present are the counselor and the client. If it is a couples' therapy or marriage therapy session, the counselor and the couple are the only people who should be present. If a minor child is undergoing counseling, often a parent is not present, but gives their consent for the session.

In today's church that tends to run rampant with concepts and ideas about various matters, it is becoming more and more common for counselors to violate the confidentiality of sessions by bringing in third-party observers to validate professionalism if accusation is brought against the leader. The counselor may leave the door open for others to hear the details of a session or may bring in a person of the same sex as the client to verify inappropriate conduct did not occur during a session. What leaders do not recognize is that such behavior is of inappropriate conduct and introduces a violated element into sessions.

It is true that disturbed or distrustful patients may bring accusation against an otherwise upstanding counselor. It is also true that there are counselors who violate clients or become inappropriately involved with their patients. All these facts, however, are irrelevant in the light of the confidential nature of counseling. The seal of confidentiality in counseling cannot be broken because of the actions or issues that could hypothetically occur. When counseling patients, untrained individuals should never be present during the session. The room is off limits to husbands, wives, family members, untrained ministry personnel, or curious onlookers. If a consultant or secondary professional is to be brought into a session for a specific purpose or reason, the counselor must receive written permission from the client. This is only to be done to better the patient's counseling care, and not for any other reason, or without authorized permission to do so.

Group counseling sessions maintain the confidentiality of the group, and those present are those with the issue or problem at hand. It must be expressively clear that what happens in the group stays in the group, and the only people present to moderate the group are trained professionals.

Reporting

The only times when confidentiality can be breached in counseling are as follows:

- A patient has threatened to kill or harm himself or herself or someone else, and the counselor has reasonable suspicion to believe it is more than a random threat.

- A counselor learns about child abuse, where a minor child is in danger. The specific details of child abuse are usually clarified within the mandated reporting laws of the state in which a counselor resides.

- A court legally mandates a counselor to reveal details of therapy as part of a court hearing or trial. This becomes relevant most often during a trial in which someone's state of mind is in question.

- If insurance is involved in payment for counselor services, a therapist may be required to report to the insurance company as evidence that therapy is required treatment for a condition.

Counselor conduct

Counselor ethics also remain consistent with their personal and professional conduct during sessions and in the interaction with a client.

It is deemed highly unethical for counselors to become personally or romantically involved with their patients. When a counselor is a pastor, apostle, or church leader, this dictates that, when counseling, the leader is not counseling a family member and is able to distinguish the line between friendship and pastoral or apostolic work. What is done as part of counseling stays in counseling, and that line is not violated under any circumstances.

Counselors should establish themselves as a trusted authority figure. Appearance is essential, with counselors appearing neat and clean, in professional attire. Face-to-face, seated counseling is often considered the most effective form of counseling, because the patient can see the counselor on a connecting level. Counselors should refrain from speaking too much and find that balance where they offer just the right amount of perspective to help the patient receive their much-needed insight. The atmosphere should be professional, with comfort. When counseling children, counselors should feel free to interact with children on their level, playing with them, if the children like.

Counselors should be observant of personal space and needed distance with clients. It is perfectly acceptable to hug or comfort a patient, within certain limits and boundaries. Those who recognize the power of healing touch know that physical contact can work as a healing agent. Physical contact, however, should not be a primary aspect of every session, nor should it be the primary focus of counseling.

Patient conduct

As important as it is for a counselor to conduct themselves with professionalism and objectivity, it is equally important that patients respect the boundaries and limits of the counselor. Patients should not intrude on the privacy of other patients, nor the privacy of the counselor. They should not be in the personal space, boundaries, property, or time of the counselor. They should recognize the relevance in a counselor's reputation and should not spread falsehoods, stories, or seek to discredit an ethical and dignified counselor.

Maintaining the dignity of the human person

Some of the wounds a counselor will see represent the deepest wounds possible to inflict or have inflicted upon a human person. A counselor must avoid judgment at all costs and respect the dignity of the human person. In the case of a victim, it is essential to give the patient a renewed sense of themselves. In the case of a perpetrator, it is essential to work with them toward seeing other people with purpose and dignity, and help them to recognize their own power to overcome the past and begin life anew, respecting boundaries and seeking forgiveness.

The dignity of the human person rests in our firm belief that God's Word teaches us we are created in His image (Genesis 1:26-27). As a result of sin, this means that people do not always live up to this image, nor do they honor the work God may be doing within and through them. What it does mean is that we honor the fact that, being created in God's image, we all have the potential to turn away from sin and turn toward God through Jesus Christ. Anything created in the image of God bears with it respect, honor, and does not deserve to be mistreated. The counselor, therefore, has the responsibility to exemplify this principle in their conduct, and honor God's ability to work within a person, as part of the counseling process.

Objectivity

Objectivity is the ability to remain objective, or neutral, in given situations. It is the professional conduct needed to keep from becoming overly emotional or attached to patients, to the point whereby we are unable to be of any help to them. This means counselors must see clients they can work with objectively. Immediate family and very close friends should be counseled by other professionals than their family members. It also means that no matter who a counselor is counseling, they must keep themselves in a particular state of purpose, operating by wisdom, rather than by emotions.

When a patient is going through the healing process, it is natural they may become emotional about things. The counselor's natural tendency may be to become emotional with them, too. Patients often have learned in their lives that emotionalism for an issue can be a basis to get attention, and, therefore, do not complete the healing process because attention becomes more valuable than healing. Counselors work to facilitate healing, not sympathy. It is essential that a counselor maintain objectivity while conveying an empathetic spirit and comforting presence. This helps the healing process continue and maintain its relevance in the life of a patient.

When counseling couples or groups, objectivity becomes especially important. A therapist cannot appear to be favoring one party over another but helping both to see essential issues for themselves and work out issues favorably. If a therapist is unable to do this due to the noncompliance of one of the parties involved, such should be noted – this is not an action against objectivity, but one of reality with an uncooperative party.

Belief in the counseling process and the ability to heal through it

If a counselor doesn't believe in the healing power present in counseling, they will be ineffective. As part of the ethics of counseling, a counselor must believe that a person can heal if they utilize it to the fullest. This is confidence in God's healing power within the counseling process. A counselor exemplifies their belief in the counseling process as they uphold its principles, its ethics, and stand behind it through the process.

Chapter Review

<u>Short Answer</u>

Answer the following questions in 1 to 3 sentences each.

- What are ethics, and why are they important in Christian counseling? What are the foundations of Christian ethics?
- When is it acceptable to breach confidentiality through a report in counseling?

CHAPTER THIRTEEN

Creating and Maintaining a Healing Atmosphere

All this I have seen and applied my mind to every deed that has been done under the sun
wherein a man has exercised authority over another man to his hurt.
- Ecclesiastes 8:9

C hristian counseling is about healing, but it is about more than just healing: it is about the honor and purpose in the process of healing. It does not approach healing as a drive-by technique or a hope of purpose that may come if one wishes hard enough for it; it approaches and recognizes that healing is a spiritual process. The counselor has the awesome privilege to travel the journey and process of healing with their client, facilitating that divine healing through the different stages of counseling. A Christian counselor will see a patient grow, transform, and develop as they watch God work and reveal in that patient's life.

Because counseling is about the healing process as much as the result, an atmosphere of healing must be always maintained during the counseling process. Maintaining such an atmosphere is not about having a certain type of lighting but about creating a sacred space where the Holy Spirit can move and flow.

The physical environment

A physical environment for counseling should be a specific place set up for counseling purposes. Many times, counselors work out of an office used for another purpose, especially if they are counseling as part of apostolic, prophetic, or pastoral ministry. The cluttered environment of a minister's workspace and working office can create an unsettled discomfort in a patient and cause them to feel the need to rush and hurry through the session. The atmosphere for counseling should be for counseling: uncluttered, clean, and open. The counselor and patient should sit across from one another, on a face-to-face level, except in the case of a child, who may need to play during session rather than sit in a chair. In the case of couples or groups, the counselor should sit in a way where everyone can be seen, and eye contact can be made. Plants or greenery (even if it is fake) should be somewhere in the atmosphere. Healing pictures, images of the Savior, and healing Scriptures should be prominent on the walls, without over-cluttering them. Pillows and blankets should be made available, as well as toys for children. Soft healing music can play, unless for some reason, it will prove to be a distraction. The atmosphere should be quiet, rather than disruptive. There should be no distractions, little noise, and a total focus on the patient at hand and their healing process.

The spiritual environment

If counseling is about the process of healing, that means counseling is a spiritual process. If we are to facilitate healing, we must create a spiritual atmosphere for healing to flow. This means we must regularly check ourselves and the spirituality flowing within ourselves. If we are Christian counselors, this means we must be Christian counselors – not New Age counselors or alternative practicing counselors. The spiritual atmosphere must be one of God, one of the Lord Jesus and revealing Himself through His types, shadows, and spiritual realities. The presence of the Holy Spirit must come through God's minister. This means that to be an effective Christian counselor, the counselor must be:

- A Christian in more than just church attendance, but one who has a true relationship with God through Christ; having a relationship that not only transforms them in and of themselves but stands as a transforming testimony to others.

- One who has a relationship with God marked by Pentecost, i.e., they operate by the indwelling of the Spirit. A Christian counselor cannot be effective if they do not believe in the Spirit's activity within our modern times, and most especially, within them and in those they counsel.

- A Christian counselor must be strong in prayer and powerful in hope. If a counselor has no hope, or lives with a pessimistic viewpoint of humanity and a person's ability to change with God's help and an alignment with His will, they will be ineffective.

- Christian counselors do not have to be perfect, nor do they have to have everything in their lives all together; but they do need to be people who seek out God and know He holds answers for various aspects of the human condition.

Christian counselors, therefore, must take the active role to pray beforehand (either before each patient or at the beginning of the day), take an active role in understanding and walking out the Scriptures, and pray with their clients for God's Spirit to remain vital and active throughout the session.

Homework and at-home activities

Counseling does not begin or end with a counseling session, formalized with a therapist. Because counseling is a process, counseling continues in between sessions, services, and events. This means that patients should be involved in activities and projects when they are at home as well as when they are in counseling session.

Counseling homework is not formalized homework that someone is graded on but consists of exercises that help to develop and build up skills that apply those principles learned in counseling. These can include journaling, prayer, application of certain spiritual gifts, Scripture studies on passages pertaining to certain issues, personal exercises in time management, scheduling, application, new behaviors and practices, and other things that help the individual in their healing process.

Incorporating spiritual gifts into healing

Just as with the concept of play therapy, some patients may have different ways by which they move and operate in healing. Freud and other psychotherapists emphasized speech and verbalization in counseling – and rightly so. Even though they may not have known the principle of life and death in the tongue found in the Word, their emphasis on speaking forth what they go through in the process of healing was an essential principle. Therapeutic response does not begin and end, however, with speech. Some people are more responsive through movement, writing, song, dance, or some other form of healing. People undergoing counseling should be encouraged to develop the different spiritual gifts they have as part of their healing process – and, in the process, to reach out to others. Whether God speaks to them through worship dance, song, prophecy, discernment, tongues, writing, encouragement, word of knowledge, word of wisdom, and so on and so forth, encourage the development of that. This establishes the individual in a purpose; in something that helps them reach out to God and bless the people of God at the same time; and continuing the process as they fully reconnect to God.

Understanding reconciliation and counseling

The Bible speaks of Jesus' ministry to reconcile humanity back to God, and to reconcile humanity one to another. The ministry of counseling is part of this agency: it seeks to reconcile people with God and reconcile them either to others or to parts of themselves damaged by others. If we see reconciliation as part of counseling, that means that Christian counselors are facilitators of a bridge to healing through reconciliation. I define reconciliation as the quiet form of deliverance ministry: it doesn't scream, doesn't shout, but it is one of the most powerful forms of deliverance there is. Reconciliation is the ultimate redemption from sin and the effects of sin, and through it, we can obtain right standing with God and engage in relationship with God and others. This means the Christian counselor has the purpose and position to walk in reconciliation: maintaining the balance between a healthy perspective of self while encouraging and engaging the client to develop a healthy sense of relationship with God and others.

Chapter Review

<u>Short Answer</u>

Answer the following question in 1 to 3 sentences.

- Explain the relationship between reconciliation and counseling.

<u>Essay Questions</u>

Construct a well-written essay (minimum 5-8 sentences), answering the following question.

- How can a Christian counselor create and maintain a healing atmosphere in counseling? Give specific examples.

CHAPTER FOURTEEN

Counseling Technique

But as for me, this mystery has not been revealed to me for any wisdom residing in me more than in any other living man, but for the purpose of making the interpretation known to the king, and that you may understand the thoughts of your mind.
- Daniel 2:30

Secular counselors tend to, as a rule, select a certain school of psychiatric theory by which they practice. While the rules are not as set in stone as they used to be, most counselors follow one school of practice over another. For example, a counselor may consider their technique to be Freudian, or Jungian, or Kleinian, with any assortment of modern beliefs or applications contained therein. Their identity as a counselor of the practice of their choosing reveals a lot about their approach to therapy, their methods and beliefs, but most importantly, what they believe to be true about therapeutic care and counseling techniques.

The same is true of the Christian counselor: how we approach the patients and the technique we use in Christian counseling reveals what we ourselves believe about therapeutic care and counseling technique.

What our counseling techniques need to say about us

- **We believe in God:** The techniques we use do not have to use "Jesus" as the first and last word of every sentence, nor do we have to recite Bible verses throughout a counseling session. As we discussed earlier in this book, the bottom line of every counseling technique we use is that it must either be a shadow of the divine, or the reality therein. Who we are and why we counsel – as well as how we counsel – must reflect our full belief in God.

- **We believe in God's ability to heal:** If a counselor doesn't believe God still heals and that God can heal, the counselor should not be in counseling. A counselor must have full assurance of faith that God is the ultimate healer. While doctors may set things or treat symptoms, the only one who truly heals is God. Counselors cannot doubt God's ability to heal, in any way, shape, or form. Counselors likewise must believe in a patient's participation in the healing process with God, receiving God's healing in their lives.

- **We believe that counseling is a means by which God heals humanity; while it is not the only means for healing, it is no less a means by which God heals:** Many Christian counselors are negative and pessimistic about counseling as a whole. They are critical of traditional psychoanalytical theory, quick to judge psychoanalytical thought, and feel that counseling, as a whole, has been a failure. Such an attitude diminishes the profession of counseling as a whole and diminishes the belief that counseling is a means by which God heals. Christian counselors need to believe God heals through counseling, and that counseling is a powerful way by which people can be healed.

- **We believe human beings are created in the image of God:** I do not question that there are many, many things wrong with humanity, all of which connect back to sin and the sinful condition of humanity. At the same time, we cannot overlook the fact that people are created in the image of God and, thereby, are worthy of respect and dignity. The Christian counselor seeks not to demoralize humanity but lift it up with the love of Christ through Christian counseling.

- **We believe in relationship with God and others via reconciliation:** It is not possible to repair every relationship in existence. Sometimes Christian counselors get so fixated on repairing relationships, they forget the essential ministry of reconciliation present in counseling. Counseling may not fix all the relationships one has had in the past, or even the ones they have in the present, but counseling can create healing, so it is possible to interact in a healthy dynamic with others from this point forward. It is also so essential that counselors do not forsake an individual's relationship with God in favor of repairing relationships. The Christian counselor can never ignore the essence of reconciling oneself with God. That may mean changes in relationships with others, or changes in one's own life in relation to others. A good Christian counselor does not omit any of these possibilities.

- **We believe people can change:** It's easy to be pessimistic about humankind. Anyone can think that humanity is a lost cause and toss it casually to the wind. The Christian counselor cannot take such a pessimistic view to humanity. Christian counselors must believe change is a choice we make as God guides us toward new decisions and behaviors in our lives. If change is impossible, Christian counseling is, too, impossible. Since we know Christian counseling can make a difference, it is essential to never nullify the very motivating factor behind Christian counseling, which is change.

The power of suggestion

Christian counselors need to understand the power of suggestion in counseling and beware themselves from ordering patients around or becoming too suggestive in counseling technique. The temptation always exists to over-offer advice or become bossy or demanding with clients, especially when a patient's situation seems to warrant what may be obvious to a counselor. In technique, remembering the power of suggestion is perhaps the most essential aspect to effective counseling technique. For hundreds of years, counseling has served to offer people a place to assess and solve various issues without judgment and without criticism. It is not the counselor's place to impose their own personal viewpoints on the client.

In considering the more dogmatic side of Christianity, it is especially relevant a Christian counselor does not allow personal viewpoints to slip into counseling technique and advice. If someone is coming for an issue pertaining to a "hot button" issue, such as homosexuality, abortion, divorce, women in ministry, or an issue with a child, it is not the counselor's place to impose their viewpoint on the individual, thereby telling them what to do. It is the counselor's place to facilitate a discovery of truth in the individual's life, using wisdom and wise application of God's Word to discover where they need to be, what they need to do, what identity of themselves they need to adopt through God's view of them, and why they may be facing a troublesome situation at this time.

Emotional distance and objectivity

Perhaps the most difficult aspect of counseling for many is maintaining a balance of emotional distance and objectivity. Counseling brings forth many issues, pains, and emotions in people. It can be a challenge for a counselor to distance themselves in the pursuit of remaining objective.

Professional distance is the ability to remain objective despite the emotionality or tumult which may arise during a counseling session. In a Christian context, referring to spiritual gifts, emotional distance and objectivity are under the spiritual gift of discernment. To operate effectively as a Christian counselor, counselors need more than just the prophetic aspect of empathy and being able to speak over people's lives; they also need to be discerning. As Christian counselors, the inclination to be shocked over something or become emotionally attached to a person in pain through counseling cannot be denied.

Emotional objectivity and distance are obtained as one steps outside of their feelings and looks pragmatically at the situation. It is very easy to understand the difference. Such brings forth not only objectivity, but also self-control and perspective to counseling. The principles of counseling are brought about by techniques that allow the individual person the ability to receive God's revelation themselves, and the technique process can't apply if we are emotionally involved. By distance, we give the client the space and needed process to figure out what they need from their situation for themselves.

There are many reasons why emotional distance and objectivity are essential for the Christian counselor, both on a practical and a spiritual level. These include:

- **There is a difference between spiritual perception and emotional involvement:** If we have learned anything from history, it is that people can be emotionally manipulated under the guise of spiritual experience. Just because something feels a certain way, makes us cry, tugs at our heartstrings, or engages us on an emotional level does not mean it is truth or reflects truth — it means it effects our emotions. In counseling, the things people tell us may raise emotions in them as well as raise such in us. Discernment lets us know mere emotion from what is a genuine spiritual experience.

- **We cannot be effective if we are emotionally involved:** Emotions have a way of clouding judgment. Much of the time, people who seek out counseling have been shaken by emotional experiences or blinded by emotions to the point where they cannot discern what they need to in order to hear from God in their specific situations. If the counselor becomes blinded by those emotions along with the client, the counselor's technique and advice are clouded and the patient is unable to utilize counseling's system to receive the objectivity needed to heal.

- **The thoughts and feelings we may have about a situation may not be those that God wishes to convey to the individual through the counseling process, at least not in the way we desire to convey it:** When I do counseling with people, I often have very definitive thoughts and feelings about a client's situation based on the information they provide. These opinions I have, however, may or may not be constructive to the situation at hand. We must separate what is constructive from what is destructive in a counseling setting, and the only way we do this is by discernment.

- **There is a difference between venting and prophecy:** Clients can become frustrating at different points in the counseling process. How we may be feeling may be correct but deciding that we should vent every frustration and feeling we have as prophecy is incorrect. Discern what is feeling from what is a word from the Lord and operate accordingly.

- **Emotionalism does not bring change, it encourages people to remain where they are:** The church's emotionalism proves that it does not help people to grow, it helps people to stay exactly where they are, flooded by emotions and thoughts about those emotions. As counselors, we are called to help people break through emotionalism to make sound, pragmatic decisions. If we ourselves are wrought with emotion over their issues, we cannot help to bring them to a place of change.

- **Not every spirit is of God:** Emotionalism can be a powerful weapon used by the enemy to draw people away from where they need to be. Becoming emotionally involved with clients can work against both the client and the therapist quickly, drawing both astray into a realm of the demonic that renders counseling totally ineffective.

- **We can't hear from God for clients if we are busy hearing from clients instead of God:** The counselor has the job to listen, but every Christian counselor has the unique position to reveal the rhema word of God to their client. That rhema word cannot be received if the counselor is blinded by emotional ties and lack of objectivity.

Understanding technique

As the author of this book, I believe Christian counseling does not hold to one technique but combines the best of all traditional techniques into one, sound system, while incorporating Christian principle and instruction into method.

In good conscience as counselors, we cannot reject the types and shadows spoken of earlier as we approach patients. We need to bring forth the best offered and incorporate that into our work. In keeping with these methods and understandings, we also need to consider the following:

- The benefit in face-to-face counseling for adults and play therapy for children.

- The importance in listening, rather than talking too much during counseling.

- Maintain power in speech, and do not resort to vulgarity or speaking things over clients that should not be said.

- Avoid judging clients for decisions, choices, orientations, lifestyles, and issues they may be, have, or have had.

- Allow the patient the space (mental and physical) to process information and develop revelation on their own.

- Do not berate the client with too much information at one time.

- Do incorporate hands-on activities into counseling as necessary.

- Never underestimate the power of prayer and Scripture, but do not force it on a patient.

- Always abide by ethics.

- Do not transfer personal issues onto clients.

- The approach to counseling must be constructive, rather than destructive.

- Counseling should not be viewed as preaching one-on-one, but as a means for revelation.

Chapter Review

Short Answer

Answer the following question in 1 to 3 sentences.

- Why are emotional distance and objectivity so essential to Christian counseling?

Infographic

Create an infographic on:

- The different things our counseling techniques need to say about us

CHAPTER FIFTEEN

The Different Phases of Counseling

To me they listened and waited,
And kept silent for my counsel.
After my words they did not speak again,
And my speech dropped on them.
They waited for me as for the rain,
And opened their mouth as for the spring rain.
I smiled on them when they did not believe,
And the light of my face they did not cast down.
I chose a way for them and sat as chief,
And dwelt as a king among the troops,
As one who comforted the mourners.
- Job 29:21-25

Although not a common aspect taught in counseling circles, those who undergo counseling go through different phases of development through the counseling process. It's important for a Christian counselor to recognize the potential pitfalls and issues that may arise as part of the counseling experience. The pitfalls which may occur come through the different phases of counseling and are so important that we cannot help but note them. It is the same principle as the concept of a book having a beginning, a middle, and an end. To complete a counseling process, a patient must pass through different phases, moving from beginning, to middle, to end. his proves that God's work of order is still present within counseling, because it is a work of creation. As a person walks through the stages of counseling, they become a new creature in Christ, yet again. This work is unto the saving victory of Jesus Christ this side of heaven: the triumph over ailments and issues unto a place of reconciliation, deliverance, and healing.

These three phases of counseling can come forth in one session, over a few sessions, or over several sessions. One client may transition between the different phases quickly, while others take longer and experience many hang-ups here and there. The point is not how long the process takes, but the working of the process unto the healing of the patient. This becomes more relevant as we identify patients who may not be progressing as they should, or who seem to be falling into continual patterns of destructive behavior.

Early phase

The early phase of counseling is noted by three different stages: disorientation, acknowledgement, and first-fruits.

- **Disorientation** is exactly what it sounds like: a phase in which a client recognizes they are living with an issue or in a state of being that is counter to orientation, or God's order. They are, in common speak, "off balance" somewhere. They seek out a counselor for their healing, reaching out for help. Disorientation is a difficult time for a patient. They realize something they are often not understanding and may be closed, distrusting, and uncooperative. For a patient to break through with the counselor, the counselor must exhibit a consistent pattern of behavior with the client, reflecting patience and empathy. It is important the counselor establish trust with the client, refraining from criticism or judgment.

- **Acknowledgement**, also known as awakening, is the stage of counseling by which the counseling process begins to bring revelation to the client. While not quite understanding where it will take them, acknowledgement brings the patient to a place of realization, aware of what is going on within them, and of the necessary changes that must take place.

- **First-fruits** is a term referring to the first part of a harvest or profit. In the case of counseling, first-fruits are the first signs of breakthroughs with a patient. It is the first harvest of the labor of counseling. Prior to this stage, counseling is very counselor-driven, rather than patient driven. The counselor works to draw the patient out of himself or herself and to a place where victory is possible. In comparison with the amount of work that needs to be done, the first-fruit stage may seem insignificant, but it is not. This harvest brings the patient to a place where ultimate victory is possible. It is an essential aspect of encouragement in counseling's revelation process. It is also an important step in the relationship between counselor and client, because it notes a breakthrough of trust and confidence as both move the client toward the next level of healing.

Middle phase

- **Growth** is a stage marked by a desire to move forward in the counseling process. Having received a first-fruits harvest, the client pushes forward. They may move fast or slow, or desire growth faster than it seems to come. The client is heavily engaged in the process, seeking any possible way to move forward. Growth is a stage noted by enthusiasm. We should not mistake genuine enthusiasm for results, however. The desire in growth is to grow, and this means the counselor must work with the client to see the results the client desires. This is the first sign of a client-driven process, where the counselor begins to serve as a facilitator of the client's direction rather than a moderator of the overall experience. During growth, the counselor must guide and direct, while the client pursues.

- **Empowerment** is noted by a sense of power that comes from the Lord through the process. It is a burst of spiritual stamina helping the client to pursue through to see the desired results from the process thus far. Growth motivates, and empowerment provides endurance. The journey from start to end can be difficult, and through empowerment, a client receives their full need to continue to the end.

- **Development** is the visible sign of growth in a patient. A developing patient is a patient who is working through issues and moving toward victory. This stage is marked by better communication and productive behaviors. While there may still be issues, the patient is reaching a point where they are visibly able to see the result of their product and are benefiting from the good results of counseling.

Latter phase

- **Orientation** is the opposite of disorientation. A patient will never be perfect, as is true of all human beings, but the stage marked by overwhelm, confusion, and distrust has passed. The patient is assured of the healing power in the counseling process and understands how to better deal with both the negatives and positives of life. Feelings and experiences of disorientation, such as anger, confusion, frustration, stress, and strife are all a part of life and must be handled appropriately. Techniques learned in counseling help the patient to better understand why they have gone through what they have, and how they can deal with negatives in the future. Counseling is an important bridge between disorientation and orientation because many clients will have lived with disorientation so long, they will not know how to handle orientation. Positive feelings of orientation, such as order, stability, and contentment are also an adjustment, and require new ways of thinking and interacting with the world. The transition provided by counseling help bridge the gap between one way of thinking and the other.

- **Contentment** is the sense of release a client feels knowing counseling has worked and the blessing of walking in victory. The client is appreciative toward the counselor for the help received and has a prepared sense of orientation that is both practical and applicable.

- **Peace** is the result of receiving healing from the counseling process. It marks the conclusion of counseling sessions, having fully equipped the individual for purpose and victory in life.

Abnormalities in the process

Not every counseling experience goes as described above. It is common for clients to get stuck in different phases of understanding or move in lateral ways to avoid moving through the different stages and phases of counseling. A client may behave in specific ways that are counter-productive to the healing process.

- **Regression**, or moving back to an earlier stage in time, is the most common abnormality in the counseling process. When regressing, a patient may begin displaying behaviors they abandoned through counseling or may return to earlier patterns or concepts of thought. Regression occurs because the counseling process becomes uncomfortable to the client, and they seek to revert back to that which is comfortable. Change isn't always fun because it means venturing out into things that are new and different; it is a new territory, so to speak. Regression does not have to be permanent, but it is important the therapist work with the client to get them back on track.

- **Transference** was traditionally taught by Freud to refer to the development of a romantic attachment toward a counselor by a client. It was not, indeed, a genuine attachment, but an illusion, or fantasy bond of one, because of the counselor's work to help and meet needs within the patient. In the process, the patient was able to receive met needs from the counselor that they were formerly unable to meet with other figures of nurturing or authority in their lives. Transference is not necessarily always romantic, nor is it always positive. Transference happens when a client transfers any set of feelings toward a counselor. They can be positive, negative, or motivated by anger, hostility, rage, or inappropriate attachment of any sort. As the counselor represents any number of images to the client, including emotional, parental, comforting, or relational, it makes emotional distance and objectivity even more relevant in the counseling process.

- **Quitting** comes about in counseling for any number of reasons. Clients may find themselves unable to pay for services, may be weary of the process, or decide moving forward is simply not what they want to do. Counselors should push clients to verbalize the reasons why they decide to quit counseling. While this decision should be respected, the counselor should provide counterpoints to the consequences of quitting counseling, which are often not considered in the decision.

Chapter Review

<u>Essay Questions</u>

Construct a well-written essay (minimum 5-8 sentences), answering the following question.

- Construct an essay about the different phases of counseling and each of the stages associated with each phase.

SECTION III

The Spirituality of
Christian Counseling

CHAPTER SIXTEEN

The Ephesians 4:11 Ministry and Counseling

And He gave some as apostles, and some as prophets, and some as evangelists, and some as pastors and teachers,
for the equipping of the saints for the work of service, to the building up of the body of Christ;
until we all attain to the unity of the faith, and of the knowledge of the Son of God, to a mature man,
to the measure of the stature which belongs to the fullness of Christ. As a result, we are no longer to be children,
tossed here and there by waves and carried about by every wind of doctrine, by the trickery of men,
by craftiness in deceitful scheming; but speaking the truth in love, we are to grow up in all aspects into Him
Who is the head, even Christ, from Whom the whole body, being fitted and held together
by what every joint supplies, according to the proper working of each individual part,
causes the growth of the body for the building up of itself in love.
- Ephesians 4:11-16

Up until this point in this book, we have examined universal characteristics applicable to all types of Christian counselors. In this chapter, we are going to look at the efficiencies and types of counseling available within leadership through the Ephesians 4:11 ministry. We know that in Christianity God has established the Ephesians 4:11 ministry as His offices for ministry execution. Recognizing the Ephesians 4:11 ministry as the official standard for God's ministers and the only recognizable offices for ministry within the church helps us learn about Christian counseling and ministry.

When a Christian gets in trouble, their first line of defense is to seek out the aid and assistance of a Christian minister, someone in the Ephesians 4:11 ministry that is either their leader or a leader that they trust. Being connected to a trusted leader is important within the Body of Christ for several reasons, but providing counsel and counseling are two of the most important. Walking in a sense of accountability and order helps to create those important connections that will assist us as we come to different points of passage throughout our lives.

For many years, Christianity has exclusively acknowledged the office of the pastor, ignoring the other gifts present in the five-fold ministry. When people seek out a leader, regardless of their purpose in ministry, they often seek the characteristics of a pastor while remaining ignorant of the fact that each office of Ephesians 4:11 contains its own specific gifts. When it comes to counseling, these different gifts make a major difference in the type of counseling and approach to counseling one may receive. The different gifts of the Ephesians 4:11 ministry exist because different types of counseling are needed within the Body of Christ, and in attempt to meet those needs, all those different counseling needs can be practically and applicably met.

Because the role of the pastor has been distorted in the attempt to make it the sole office applicable down to modern times, counseling is largely identified with the pastoral office. Associated with that identification is a specific way in which counseling is handled – the pastoral, or shepherding approach to counseling. This has given people the impression that counseling should always flow in ministry in a specific way – softly, quietly, and without push or haste – and, therefore, people are thoroughly confused when other offices of the Ephesians 4:11 ministry step up to do counseling work.

There is not adequate room in this book to describe every office of the Ephesians 4;11 ministry in thorough detail. For that I recommend reading my book specifically on Ephesians 4:11. What I am going to do instead is examine the various aspects of each office of Ephesians 4:11 that change the nature of counseling they are able to give. The apostle, prophet, evangelist, pastor, and teacher all serve a specific function and with that specific function comes the ability to counsel and guide.

The Apostle

The office of the apostle is, by far, one of the most recognized in the New Testament. In modern times, there is a great movement to try and understand the modern application of the apostle and its role in today's church. While many today believe apostles are valid for our day and age, it is debated the exact nature they are to play and their role and function within the modern church. In this process, the apostle often gets misconstrued with any host of other offices, especially the prophet and the pastor. It's also a misconception to assume the apostle is all five offices of the five-fold rolled into one. There are five separate, unique, and distinct offices in the five-fold for a reason, and each have their own purpose. The apostle, as part of the five-fold, is no different. The office holds its own unique, special, and appointed purpose within the Body of Christ.

The apostle is "one who is sent." This tells us many things about the type of leader an apostle is. For one, the apostle is called to go forth with the Gospel, with the news of Jesus' resurrection and the grace of the Gospel to the world. The apostle is sent forth to go first, to go before others, as a leader and pioneer in any number of ways to build up the Kingdom of God. An apostle may be sent to a specific nation or nations, territories, ethnic groups, churches, regions, or have a very specific apostolic purpose within the Body of Christ (such as training up leaders through a university or through apostolic covering). The apostle's work is accomplished through preaching, teaching, establishing, planting, growing, and working. Overall, we can see in the New Testament that the work of the apostle was a call to build up the church by building up church leaders. In being sent with the Gospel revelation, the apostle can lead, guide, and edify the church's leaders in a unique way among five-fold leaders.

Because the apostle works with leaders, apostolic counseling is a form of leadership counseling. The apostle's job in counseling is to set, establish, and bring forth order. Apostolic leadership counseling is extremely direct, and often brutally honest. Counseling leaders with various issues is radically different than helping a church member without a ministry call. The reason for this is obvious: one walking in a ministry call or developing a ministry call is required to walk in a certain level of standard, which means overcoming minor issues that may be of major issue to someone else. If someone is genuinely preparing for a life in ministry or already operating in ministry, they can't be easily overcome by the issues of life that distract from call and purpose. For this reason, apostolic counseling is a bit "harder" on the individual than normal, nominative counseling. The apostle seeks to bring the leader to the full place of power within their office and recognizes this will not happen if people are "babied."

Apostolic counseling also relates to extensive advice, study, and guidance on spiritual and leadership matters. Their exacting nature, personality, and insight guides the leader or leader-in-training to the exact place they need to be in the pursuit of great leadership. The apostle is strongest in the area of counsel, provided for leadership discipline and necessary working. This also makes an apostle a leader in relational counseling, offering perspective on relationships and on interactions with one another. The apostle's perspective is going to be different than another leader, however. The apostle is going to provide advice that helps set an individual on their correct course with God and prepare the individual for the changes that will cause in their relationship with others. The apostle does not encourage one to back down from a calling but provides the individual with tools to help deal with the rejections, disappointments, and offenses incurred upon them by others who don't understand the calling at hand.

An apostle is also a great counselor in the area of discerning a calling. When someone is looking to discern a call from God, a great place to go is to an apostle. The call of the apostle helps to bring discernment, advice, and guidance to one who is seeking God in a deeper way about how to serve Him in this life. The apostle can help guide someone to educational information or training, preparations for ordination, and other essential aspects for ministry training. Every apostle should be interested in developing scholarship, character, integrity, qualification, and seeing fruit come about from those who seek work and office in the five-fold ministry.

The most difficult thing for an apostle to step back and pray about in counseling is the relational aspect between humanity and personal issues. Apostles are known for complex and exacting standards of others. If one is not careful, an apostle can run the risk of being a little too harsh and impractical in their standards of others. The apostle expects their clients to step up and face things with confidence, grace, and the Spirit of God. If you are looking for sympathy or pity, an apostle is not a good candidate as a counselor. An apostle is going to tell it to you like it is and is going to give the necessary direction to solve a problem. Apostles have developed their wisdom and understanding from years of experience as they walk through the various challenges and issues others face. Having that hands-on experience and continually dying to self gives the apostle a unique perspective to be able to lead others, as they have literally had God lead them through all things themselves.

The Prophet

The office of the prophet is known both in the Old Testament. In terms of counseling, the prophetic office has been known for its objective counsel and wise guidance since the beginning of time. Because counseling is a part of the charismatic prophetic gift available to the entire body of believers, those who walk in the office of the prophet also walk in this prophetic gift. Of all offices of the Ephesians 4:11 ministry, the prophet offers a unique perspective on counseling that can be beneficial to both leaders and lay members of the church alike.

A prophet is a person who speaks the words of God. There are a few ways a prophet may do this. Some prophets work strongly in education, training other prophets in prophetic ministry (not how to be a prophet, but the ins and outs of prophetic work). Some prophets are powerful preachers and teachers who also bring forth a word of knowledge or wisdom. Some prophets are powerful in seeing future events and being able to proclaim God's revealed word over nations, regions, churches, and people. Some prophets are powerful in the area of writing, and others in teaching specific matters of prophetic interpretation pertaining to both the Scriptures and events throughout the Word and history. Some prophets are all of the above, or parts of the above. Even though prophets may operate through various prophetic gifts, all prophets have the clear job to do what they do for three purposes: reveal God's will to the people, call people to repentance, and to encourage the righteous. They also operate heavily in the discernment of spirits, spiritual gifts, and act as guardians of the church. More often than not, the job of the true prophet emphasizes repentance, the will of God, and discernment. The prophetic office is one of heavy correction, revealing the purposes, plans, and call of God to turn from sin, even when people have turned from visible sin but may harbor covered sins or have repented from some sin, but not all sin in their lives. The prophet has a difficult job that is often intensified as they hear from God, receive revelation, and "pick up" on various spiritual issues present both within the church and within individuals who cross their paths.

While it may seem like prophets are free agents, the Bible teaches that the apostle and prophet are called to work together to form the foundation of the church (Ephesians 2:20). The prophet and apostle provide balance and purpose for one another. For this reason, apostles and prophets are the ministry offices responsible for leadership development within the church. While modern religious movements have entrusted this responsibility to the pastor, that is not the work assigned to the pastor. This means prophets do not just speak arbitrarily to people here and there, they speak as God assigns them – to both leaders through correction and edification and to the general body of Christ.

The prophet's job in counseling is to bring forth revelation. Prophetic counseling can be either for leaders or for the laity. This means a prophet is strongly anointed to do either. This makes a prophet a powerful counselor when addressing issues that affect general life and ministry life. The prophet's most powerful gifting is that of empathy. The prophet can both identify with how the individual is feeling and how God perceives the situation by revelation. They are good for counsel, guidance, relationship issues, leadership, discernment, and encouragement. Depending on the circumstance at hand, a prophet's advice may vary. The prophet will encourage a leader to discern a call and will also have unique perspective on the challenges and things that hold that leader back. The prophet's advice may come through a word, a prophecy, or practical, down-to-earth guidance, but will be very spiritually driven, with a strong emphasis on the individual's call from God and relationship to God.

By nature, prophets tend to be very emotional and moody people. This means the prophet's major pitfall when counseling will be the temptation to become emotionally involved with a client. The prophet may lose perspective and discernment in a sympathetic pursuit, thus causing them not to be objective. The prophet's responsibility in counseling is to develop empathy (a sense of intellectual identification with a problem or issue) rather than sympathy (taking the issue upon themselves emotionally). Prophets also frustrate easily and tend to be withdrawn. It is essential the prophet learns to discern their own issues, perspectives, and thoughts in a given situation from those of God. Prophets develop their advice and expertise through divine revelation, which means the spiritual work of a prophet will be of important relevance within a counseling setting.

The Evangelist

The evangelist's work is to "proclaim Christ." This means the heart of everything the evangelist does is bringing people to Christ: the unsaved, the mediocre in their faith, and the one with a knowledge of God, but without a proper development of faith and relationship. Most do this through preaching, evangelistic work, social work that reaches out to meet needs in the community and areas where they are, itinerant travelling ministry, and sometimes, writing. Everything about the evangelist's call is Christ-centric, from outreach to preaching. In keeping with this task, the evangelist's central focus in Christian counseling is Christ.

Evangelistic counseling is not appropriate for everyone at every stage of the journey with God. It is a specific area of counseling that relates to the individual's relationship with Christ and examining various pitfalls in the human condition that can be resolved in exploring a deeper relationship with Him. Its Christ-centered nature is different than the presence of Christ in apostolic or prophetic counseling. While apostolic counseling seeks to set structure and prophetic counseling seeks to bring revelation, the evangelist's counseling seeks to bring forth the reality of the nature and person of Christ. This means through an evangelist's counseling, the client receives a better understanding of Christ in their lives, His presence, His purpose, His plan of salvation, and how they can walk out Christ's plan in their lives. This means that those who benefit most from an evangelist's counseling are those who are new believers, believers seeking a better walk with the Lord or seeking direction in their relationship with Him, or those who need to make Jesus Christ more of a central focus in their lives. This can be both independent or relational, as a Christ-centered relationship approach can benefit both individuals and couples or families. On a larger scale, the work of the evangelist helps believers understand how to interact and live the Gospel one to another.

The evangelist also excels in counseling others how to better be witnesses of the Gospel and spread the Gospel better in their own lives. Most believers today would admit most of the church lacks in the areas of evangelism and witnessing, with the principle of social gospel work all but disappearing all together. These essential aspects of church and ministry can be restored and upheld as the evangelist counsels both members and the church at large in how to reinstate such a heart and attitude and proper ways to implement these important aspects of ministry and life into our spiritual understanding once again.

The most difficult aspect of counseling for an evangelist is two-fold. Evangelists tend to be very social by nature, and discussion may lose its counseling aspect, rather turning to nominal conversation without the necessary details and edge of counseling. The second aspect is interest. The evangelist is a go-getter by nature, interested in movement and winning souls. The disciplines needed for regular counseling can become boring to the evangelist after a while, especially if the same issues come up over and over again. As the evangelist cuts to repentance and instructs Christ in the word and in the world, an evangelist may also become impatient and short at times with clients. It is essential the evangelist stay connected to other offices of the five-fold ministry and connected with the church and keep their own relationship with Christ central to them and Christ central to counseling experience at all times.

The Pastor

The office of the pastor is the most visible ministry office, both worldwide and throughout history. It is also the most universally misunderstood. The job of the pastor is to care for, guide, and shepherd (as the word "pastor" means "shepherd") the local congregation of the saints. It is not the job of the pastor to train leaders beyond those maybe needed on a local church level, oversee multiple congregations, or operate as apostles or prophets while serving as pastors. In this crazy modern pursuit to create pastors who mimic five offices in one, the true beauty of the pastoral office has been lost. Along with its lost general purpose is a loss in understanding pertinent to the pastor's role in counseling.

The pastor's primary job is to love and care for the people of God. Most of the time, a true pastor's call is to lead the people of the church who do not have a formal ministry call, also called the laity. The pastor's ministry work is to keep these people in the faith, teaching, nurturing, and growing them to discover God's call for them in this world. The pastor's role is essential because, in the scope of numbers, most of the church will never be called to church leadership. Because of this, pastors are called to be shepherds, appointed and installed by apostles, receiving the revelation of the prophet, and helping to lead those whose hearts have been focused and centered on Christ by the evangelist.

Pastors teach (both verbal and writing), preach, lead, guide, correct, and encourage those they follow. As in keeping with the role of the shepherd, the pastor has the responsibility to see those under his or her care do not go astray into false teaching. This means pastoral counseling centers on guidance. It is a more moderate form of counseling: while apostolic and prophetic counseling are noted for intensity and evangelistic counseling noted for centering, the pastor's counseling seeks to guide people to the truth of faith, the abundant life of Jesus Christ and their place within God's Kingdom.

Pastoral counseling is about meeting the needs of the people, ranging from issues within their relationship to God, to overcoming personal problems, to relationship problems with others, to spiritual battles, to issues present with understanding teaching, to loss and grief, and beyond. For this reason, pastors should be trained in a wide variety of areas to meet the needs of the people, including grief ministry, marriage counseling, personal counseling, and spiritual education. In pastoral counseling, it is essential the pastor conveys his or her love for the person or people receiving counseling. Love does not mean the pastor approves of the behavior or issues of the person in question, but it does mean the pastor does not judge that individual. Through a heart of loving compassion, a pastor should convey a sense of understanding and truth, helping the individual to go through rather than remain stuck. By doing this, the pastor conveys a sense of hope. When discipline is needed, the pastor exercises needed discipline as an opportunity to teach and implement a sense of self-discipline in the individual. The protective nature of the pastor can also be seen in counseling, as the pastor works to guard the individual from error by corrective behavior.

The pastor's heart for his or her people is what also makes counseling difficult for them. The temptation exists for the pastor to become overly sympathetic and emotionally attached to those he or she counsels. Pastors need to remember their purposes in counseling of people are growth and development. Pastors also need to maintain the balance between sympathy and tyranny. It's not the pastor's place to become a dictator, nor is it their place to let people have their way all the time. In keeping with love, the pastor represents a loving authority, one that disciplines out of love and loves with everything they have. It's important pastors stay connected to apostles, prophets, and evangelists for balance: to discuss issues that they may be having with counseling and pastoring in general, and to see a missed perspective or a needed balance in technique.

The Teacher

Last but not least, the office of the teacher is perhaps the most unrecognized office in the modern church. With the disappearance of Sunday school and weekly church classes, the concept of a teacher within the church has all but been abandoned. This doesn't mean the teacher is irrelevant, however. The Bible gives prominent place to teaching and its relevance in both the Old Testament community of believers and the New Testament church. Teaching is a means by which the truth is disseminated throughout the Body of Christ and is presented on a scholarly and apologetics level to non-believers as well. The office of the teacher reaches every level of the church, from child through adult, and reaches outward by presenting the beliefs and doctrines of the church on an educational level.

The teacher serves to, simply put, teach. They may teach any level of the church through instruction or may write apologetically or instructionally. This means the teacher's role in both general ministry work and in counseling is directive.

A teacher is not often an office one thinks of in terms of counseling. Even in the secular arena, teachers aren't considered sources for counseling. This, however, is a misnomer. What makes a teacher an effective teacher is also what makes them an effective counselor. When instruction is needed one-on-one in a specific area, a teacher is a great place to go. It is no different when it comes to matters of a spiritual nature. If someone seeks clarification on a doctrinal issue or on how a spiritual subject affects someone's life, a teacher is the person to seek out. The direct nature of teaching makes it understandable and applicable in any way needed to that person.

The directness of the teacher can also be its downfall when it comes to counseling. Teachers often teach larger audiences, which means they handle matters succinctly and to-the-point. It may be difficult for a teacher to elaborate on a subject they already feel has been clarified. The direct nature of a teacher may also be perceived as being short or intolerant, even though that is not the case. Teachers need to wary themselves against impatience, and also thoroughly investigate any issue they do not have clarity on before presenting it in counseling.

How the five-fold ministry works together through counseling

God has given us the Ephesians 4:11 ministry for the benefit of the church. It's a myth that a genuine Ephesians 4:11 ministry leader operates ministry for themselves or to profit from ministry. Each office of the Ephesians 4:11 ministry exists to meet a need that exists in the church. In today's church, we need leadership, relational, order, revelatory, Christ-centric, pastoral, compassionate, and directive guidance in counseling. The Ephesians 4:11 ministry provides all of this, and more, giving the church a complete means to edify and build the church up. In counseling, this means the Ephesians 4;11 ministry can meet every counseling need that arises, both among the laity and the leadership alike.

Chapter Review

<u>Essay Questions</u>

Construct a well-written essay (minimum 5-8 sentences), answering the following question.

- Write an essay on the Ephesians 4:11 ministry and the way each office of Ephesians 4:11 contributes to the counseling needs of the church.

CHAPTER SEVENTEEN

Spiritual Disciplines in Christian Counseling

Then a shoot will spring from the stem of Jesse,
And a branch from his roots will bear fruit.
The Spirit of the LORD will rest on Him,
The spirit of wisdom and understanding,
The spirit of counsel and strength,
The spirit of knowledge and the fear of the LORD.
And He will delight in the fear of the LORD,
And He will not judge by what His eyes see,
Nor make a decision by what His ears hear;
But with righteousness He will judge the poor,
And decide with fairness for the afflicted of the earth;
And He will strike the earth with the rod of His mouth,
And with the breath of His lips He will slay the wicked.
Also righteousness will be the belt about His loins,
And faithfulness the belt about His waist.
- Isaiah 11:1-5

Earlier in this book, we looked at the various charismatic gifts involved in counseling. In the last chapter, we examined the five-fold ministry and counseling. Having looked at the different types of counseling one will experience through the five-fold ministry, we are now going to look at the spiritual disciplines needed for Christian counselors of every variety. Not all Christian counselors are in formal church leadership, and not every Christian counselor who practices a form of Christian counseling is part of the Ephesians 4:11 ministry. There are many qualified, professional Christian counselors who simply acknowledge a call to help others through Christian counseling. Spiritual disciplines enable a Christian counselor to function both through spiritual gift and discipline unto a ministry of healing through counseling.

Six gifting attributes from the Holy Spirit

I have discussed in diverse places throughout this book the connection between counseling and the prophetic gift of God's people. While prophets are a leadership role designated of the Ephesians 4:11 ministry, the gift of prophecy – or being able to prophecy through a word, instruction, or vision – is available to the entire body of Christ as a charismatic gift. Under the heading of prophecy are many varied gifts, all prophetic in nature, that enhance the counseling call and experience as a Christian counselor works God's revelation through counseling.

Prior to the Charismatic gifts listed in 1 Corinthians 12 and Romans 12, we learn about six gifting attributes that come forth from the Spirit of God, and the results of those gifting attributes. They are spoken of as emanating from the Spirit of God and resting upon Someone (and, by extension, those who are found to be in that Someone), thereby that individual and those found in that individual also receiving the qualities therein. These attributes and the results are found in Isaiah 11:2 in a Messianic prophecy. If we carefully read this prophecy, it does pertain to Jesus in the first coming but details the righteous leadership of Jesus Christ at the second coming. It also gives us insight into the servants of the Messiah who function under a leadership capacity. To lead rightly and with justice, we find the six gifting attributes from the Holy Spirit that pertain in a special way to those who lead others. As we can see from the results of these gifts, they are especially relevant in counseling. These gifts are wisdom, understanding, counsel, strength, knowledge, and fear of the Lord.

If we properly understand the gifting attributes of the Holy Spirit, they are more than just gifts: they are disciplines that guide a leader to step up and lead rightly. As disciplines, they are things a Christian counselor must work to counsel effectively, upholding the ethics of the office in a spiritual context as well as in a practical one. In the context of Christian counseling, a Christian counselor must exercise these gifts, disciplining themselves by them, to bring about an effective and powerful result from Christian counseling.

Wisdom

We spoke of the charismatic gift manifest in the "word of wisdom" earlier in this book. While a word of wisdom is something someone may receive for a specific moment or circumstance, wisdom is a longer-term application. Wisdom is practical application of God's Word in a way that changes life. By wisdom, we have good judgment, the ability to foresee the results of future decisions, and a perspective only God can give us. When we walk in wisdom, God is giving us the ability to see a situation as He would have us see it so we can implement judgment, fairness, and practical application. It is the checking of an individual's self, their perspectives, opinions, attitudes, concepts, and thoughts, allowing God to guide whoever needs leading or counseling through them.

It is unfortunate that, in the circumstance of leadership and especially counseling, many Christian leaders and counselors use their positions to be suggestive rather than wise. All-too-often, Christian counseling becomes a platform to drill a certain set of beliefs or doctrinal positions into a person's mind. If we truly understand counseling from a wise perspective, we recognize Christian counseling's power of revelation rather than indoctrination. In counseling, we are called to give wise advice, wise perspective, and lead the client in wisdom. This means we facilitate thought, the ability for the client to make their own decisions, and to develop wisdom in their own lives.

Understanding

Understanding is a big word that is not used much today. While the world talks about tolerance, it eliminates the principle of understanding all together. The reason for this is simple: understanding requires an emptying of the self and one's personal perspectives, while tolerance does not demand such. In understanding, one empties themselves of their biases and allows God to educate them in the truth of a matter. Understanding helps develop compassion while imparting the truth about a situation, individual, or other matter so a person can provide what is needed in each circumstance. It is the meeting of knowledge, wisdom, and compassion, all in one. By understanding, a Christian counselor can both understand the problem a patient is having and see the hope for a solution.

Understanding is a dual process. It comes from both research and revelation. A Christian counselor should be current with different issues and fronts of Christian counseling and other trends and should also be receiving revelation from God on the way current issues and trends affect people's lives. Understanding reflects the relevance of being a here-and-now person. Anyone can claim to uphold Biblical principle by literalizing it in a way that has no application to the issues people now face. The reality of Christian life – and especially Christian counseling – is that this is not the world it once was. The issues of old (and yes, there were issues) have either been magnified or replaced by new issues. We cannot keep trying to approach things in the exact same way that people did in days gone by. Just as we apply the Bible must adjust to include new issues and understandings, so too does the way we dispense advice and approach issues and situations. This is not a compromise of God's Word, it is growth in applying the Word through understanding. It is by this means that we see the Holy Spirit alive and active, continually helping us through every age to see God's Word applicable and as an appropriate solution to every issue now through the time when Jesus comes back.

This also means that sometimes God's Word is silent on certain issues or requires us to understand the Word in a context other than literal much of the time. Issues such as polygamy were, at one time, permissible in culture, but are no longer such today. This means that, no matter how permissible it may have seemed under the reign of King David, it is not something that is permissible in modern culture. The covering of a woman's head in Genesis identified her as a prostitute, while covering a woman's head in Corinth signified modesty. Cultural changes require a re-ordering of aspects of the Scriptures that are either silent or specific to a time and culture. If we do not approach the Word in this way, that means we will not walk in understanding. Understanding helps us to be able to help others and walk by the transforming power of the Holy Spirit rather than operate as punitive lawgivers.

The Christian counselor will be ineffective without understanding, because understanding gives the patient the opportunity to be empowered by the Spirit and aided by the counselor. If a Christian counselor does not step aside to understanding, counseling will be unfruitful.

Counsel

Counsel, and its variants, is what this book is about. Counsel is the ability to give advice. In a Scriptural understanding, we understand counsel to be more than just about giving a human's advice. Anyone can run around and give voice to their opinion about various matters. We see this quite evident in our modern times, as our society and especially internet society give opportunity for people to voice their opinions. This is a forum-driven approach to life: people approach life as a forum, and feel it is both appropriate and acceptable to say whatever they like at any point in time. This is contrary to order and also diminishes the concept of counsel as a gift. While people may have opinions about things and may even convey those opinions in the context of advice, that does not mean their opinions reflect the truth or concept of counsel. This also means people must be discerning in the acceptance of advice and in giving advice.

A counselor uses the counseling process to convey counsel to their clients. In the Christian counseling application, the counselor conveys the practical application and wisdom of God's Word to the situation a person may be in through the counseling process. This comes about through any of the varied methods we have discussed throughout this book. Sometimes it involves direct advice, but often it involves the power of bringing an individual to a place where they can realize certain things and make decisions for themselves.

Strength

Strength is a common topic discussed by many varied sources today. It is, however, a very confused topic because strength has more than one application. There is the context of physical strength, by which a person is considered weak or strong. Physical strength is measured by endurance, or the ability one must last in various physical states. Emotional, mental, psychological, and spiritual endurance are comparative in concept to physical strength: their measure is by endurance, and the ability one must last in situations of test or trial.

It is likely that an individual comes to counseling due to a weakness in their lives. The nature of the weakness can be severe and obvious, or it can be something more subtle. The reason the individual is drawn to counseling is because the counseling process offers strength in their weakness. It is the counselor's position to emphasize the healing process of strength rather than emphasizing weakness as a failure. As human beings, every one of us has weaknesses. That is why the Apostle Paul emphasized that power is perfected in weakness. The counseling process offers a perfection of strength that manifests as God works through weakness to create strength.

Knowledge

Knowledge is learning, being able to learn as God enables, being able to apply learning, and being able to interact through learning as knowledgeable. This sounds complicated, but it is not as difficult as it sounds. Knowledge is most definitely a visible discipline, something that comes about as someone applies themselves to learning. This indicates knowledge is acquired: it is not something that just happens. For a person to acquire knowledge, they must pursue learning.

God calls the Christian counselor to knowledge. This means a Christian counselor must be appropriately trained. No matter how good a Christian may seem at dispensing advice, they still need to apply themselves to proper learning so they can exude knowledge through counseling. The purpose of this is two-fold. The first reason is so the counselor can be thoroughly equipped for the purpose of counseling. The second reason is to exude the relevance of learning and knowledge in life. As believers, our desire to learn should never cease. If an individual stops learning, they stop growing and seeing different ways to approach the various issues that arise throughout life and spiritual development. Counseling with knowledge helps people to discover the relevance of knowledge in their own lives, giving something that cannot be given by directive advice.

Fear (awe) of the Lord

The word "fear" has come to have a negative connotation in common English vernacular. The word "fear" in the context of "fear of the Lord" means a sense of reverence, awe, or reverential awe. It is to consider the position of oneself in humility next to the incredible being and power found in God, our Creator. Fear of the Lord is essential as a counseling discipline because it comes about as we watch God work, time and time again, just by being Who He is. The more we are in awe of God, the more we understand the importance of what we do in counseling. As was stated earlier in this book, it is not possible to be effective in counseling if one does not believe in the healing power present in the process. Fear of the Lord brings a counselor back to the realization that the healing present in counseling truly comes from God, and no one else. If a Christian counselor fears God, they have the proper order and perspective in their lives to help others. In this process, clients also learn how to fear the Lord and how honoring God in their own lives can transform the situations they are facing.

The results – and why they are important

One of the major reasons why this book is reexamining the work of Christian counselors is because Christian counseling is nothing without results. It is true that not every Christian counseling session, client, or patient will bear the results a Christian counselor hopes for. There will always be some who do not heed and do not move forward. However, Christian counseling needs to be an effective, operative method of counseling those who need solid perspective, hope, healing, and advice.

In order to see results, Christian counselors must apply the above disciplines. It isn't enough to theorize Christian counseling; the principles behind it must be lived and applied. We learn in Isaiah 11:3-5 the results of applying disciplines to our practice:

- **Delighting in the fear of the Lord:** Walking in the fear of the Lord is nothing if we do not truly delight in what we discover about our God. The delight of the fear of the Lord occurs when we pass from people of theory about God to people truly transformed and walking with God in our day-in, day-out experience. It makes a difference when we truly delight in Who God is and this displays through our approach to counseling. It helps us approach the experience with a sense of excitement rather than dread.

- **Not judging by what eyes see:** It's easy to judge things by how they appear on the surface. The purpose of counseling is to break through the surface façade that often damages lives and hurts people long-term. Just because a marriage has been together for a long period of time doesn't mean it is a good marriage or a happy one. Just because a minister seems to have it all together doesn't mean they don't have issues. Just because a church is big does not mean the church has its problems. Just because children seem adjusted does not mean other things are not happening in their lives. Christian counseling is about the development of depth in people's lives and realizing that life is not just about what happens on the surface.

- **Not deciding by what ears hear:** On the show *House, M.D.*, the infamous Dr. House used to say, "Everybody lies." People tell us things all the time that are not necessarily true. Counseling is about more than just what people say, it is about what they do and what they become.

- **Judging by righteousness for the poor:** Most assume this means doing right by those who are economically or financially poor. While that connotation certainly can be understood, the Word of God gives us the insight that there is more than one way to be poor. A person can be poor in spirit, poor in health or emotions, poor in spiritual state, or lacking in some way, thereby being assessed as poor. A righteous judgment means taking all available information into perspective, considering that which is known as well as that which is unknown, and working for the purpose of helping someone rather than punitively punishing them. The Christian counselor, therefore, is called to work in righteousness, properly assessing every situation for those who are poor in some areas of their lives, helping through Christian counseling.

- **Deciding with fairness for the meek:** Earlier in this chapter we recognized one of the disciplines of a Christian counselor is strength. One of the reasons a Christian counselor needs to be strong is because they will encounter many weaknesses in clients and patients. Being fair is an essential quality for a good leader, and especially of a good counselor. Christian counselors will often hear various sides of a story or circumstance and must remain objective, deciding fairly how a situation can come about to best benefit both or all parties involved. This also means we must respect the principle of meekness, which we could classify as hidden strength. Just because someone is quiet or seemingly unassuming does not mean they are weak. It is important when assessing fairness, we are fair to everyone involved, especially those who do not wear their feelings, positions, or thoughts on their sleeves.

- **Striking the earth with the rod of the mouth:** There's a lot of ways this statement can be perceived. In the perception of Christian counseling, it means we need to make sure our words mean something. We should not just talk to fill space, fill uncomfortable silence, or to hear ourselves talk. When a Christian counselor speaks, the words spoken should bring change, empowerment, and purpose.

- **Slaying the wicked with the breath of the lips:** The principle of justice should resonate heavily with a Christian counselor. Our sense of justice should reflect in our speech. The work of counseling in and of itself casts down the principles of darkness, as can our words. By calling out lies and both encouraging and speaking truth, a Christian counselor helps to destroy the work of the enemy.

- **Righteousness belt about the loins and faithfulness the belt about the waist:** Being belted with righteousness in the loins and faithfulness around the waist indicates preparedness for any situation. A Christian counselor must be duly prepared and protected in the most sensitive of areas for their work as a counselor. This represents the warfare present in counseling, and the battle that often follows. Christian counselors must prepare themselves against over-involvement, emotionalism, and lack of distance from their patients. At the same time, Christian counselors must maintain empathy, compassion, and understanding. Due preparation for battle, as seen here and above, ensures the Christian counselor finds the necessary balance needed for purposed counseling experience.

Chapter Review

Infographic

Create an infographic on:

- The six gifting attributes of the Holy Spirit with a brief explanation of each attribute and why they are relevant to Christian counseling.

CHAPTER EIGHTEEN

Deliverance Ministry and Counseling

He delivers the afflicted in their affliction,
And opens their ear in time of oppression.
- Job 36:15

Although seldom studied and discussed, Christian counseling is an essential aspect of deliverance ministry. Deliverance ministry, or the specific ministry work designed to set people free from various spiritual strongholds, the demonic realm, or other spiritual issues, is often thought of in one specific context, and counseling is not it. Christian counseling, however, is one of the most powerful forms of deliverance ministry available to the believer. In instances were situations do not resolve themselves with an altar call or as quickly as an exorcism, Christian counseling provides the needed path to deliverance through method, time, and perseverance.

In order to understand how a Christian counselor operates effective deliverance ministry through counseling, we must understand what deliverance is and how it applies to the Christian counselor. If we are to do this, we must empty ourselves of the limited notions we often have about deliverance ministry and recognize the principle of deliverance goes far beyond an experience had in an altar call. Some people simply need a more thorough form of deliverance than can be experienced in a few minutes. For these more complicated situations, Christian counseling provides the answer.

Understanding deliverance

In order to believe in spiritual deliverance, one must believe in the opposite of deliverance, which is spiritual captivity. When someone is released from captivity, they receive deliverance. Most people understand captivity in the sense of spiritual possession (or some description thereof), where a person is bound by an evil spirit or spirits, or demon or demons. What people believe about the realm of demonology from this point on often varies. Some people believe it is impossible for a true Christian to be demon possessed, some people believe in generational curses that follow a believer despite being saved, some people believe anyone can be possessed at any time, some people believe possession is beyond a person's realm or control of choice, some regard various issues such as drug and alcohol addiction and mental illness as possession, and some people believe the concept of possession goes beyond spirits, into the realms of past hurts, offenses, and sins. Some people believe in combinations of the above, and others reject all of it together. There are those who claim to be believers today who reject the notions of possession, captivity, and deliverance all together.

The different perspectives on deliverance tell me that much of today's church does not understand the workings of the spirit realm. The modern church understanding of deliverance and spirituality is always accompanied by a big, dramatic show instead of truth on these essential matters. If we understood the spiritual realm properly, we would better understand the ways in which the enemy works and be better prepared as to how to handle it.

Spiritual captivity is not as simple as pronouncing someone to be "possessed" or to "have a demon." While this may be a simple explanation in some instances, it is not necessarily the case for every case of spiritual captivity. Let us look, however, at the concept of "possession" for a few moments. Media sensationalism has given great visual effect to the concept of possession but has done so both inaccurately and ineffectively. To understand possession is to understand the power of demonic influence. Someone can be influenced by the power of God through the Holy Spirit, or someone can be influenced by the power of the demonic through the devil or one of his angels, known as a demon. Simply put, possession is when one is acting, interacting, behaving, and affecting others as they are influenced and guided by demonic power. Many times, the demonic realm operates more quietly than loudly, and can come, influence, and depart by any number of means. Someone who is possessed may exhibit any number of symptoms, ranging from dramatic to sublime, or seemingly none at all. It is true that anyone can become possessed. This is not cause for alarm or fear, but a simple statement that as long as people are sinners, they can become influenced by the demonic realm. If one is walking with God in the way they need to and living filled with the Holy Spirit, demonic possession does not become a concern in the same way it does when someone is not obedient to God. If one is only walking with God when it is convenient, the nominal, disobedient believer (even if only occasional) will encounter a risk of demonic possession. When one is possessed, they are captive of Satan. The operation of Satan is the counterfeit of God, because both operate through the will of human beings. Just as one operates for God by aligning their will to His, one can operate for Satan by aligning their will with the enemy.

It is also possible to be captive to oneself. I often refer to this as a "middle place" between the demonic and divine. This happens when a person is what is commonly classified as selfish or self-centered. It is obvious that when one becomes so preoccupied with self, they become agents of the enemy. There are many ways, however, to be captive to oneself. Someone can be captive by personal sin, captive by their emotions or haunts of memories, or in captivity due to illness, or held bound by personal opinions or convictions that are leading the person into a negative place in life. In keeping with this, one can also be in captivity due to the consequences of the sins of others, or in captivity by circumstances created by someone else.

Despite the cause or origin of captivity, one needs to be set free from any captivity they may experience. We know in the Word that Jesus came to set the captives free. This does not mean every single person He came to set free is demonically possessed, nor does it mean someone can't become demonically possessed after they have been set free. It simply means that those who are bound by something, whether it is spiritual, emotional, physical, cultural, financial, personal, or inflicted, can be set free. That is the heart of deliverance ministry — walking in a ministry that seeks to set people free by the power of God. To effectively operate in deliverance ministry, one must get past the notion that it is only about demonic possession, as well as the concept that everything that happens to someone is due to possession. Deliverance is about being set free, no matter what form captivity takes.

Christian counseling as a deliverance ministry

Traditional deliverance ministry is regarded as a fast-paced altar call experience. It is often noted for drama and grandeur. A minister versed in deliverance ministry may scream, shout, spit, shake, jump over things, or even become physical with a person in attempt to get a demon out of a person, whether that person always has a demon, or not.

Counseling is often not considered because it is quiet and undramatic. It is also considerably more involved and long-term than a deliverance session at the altar. It is sad to say that many ministers and even people in need of deliverance today seek a "quick fix" to problems. The persistence needed to change hearts, minds, and situations is often not an aspect considered in deliverance ministry. If a person can't get what they need at the altar, the person is thought to be resistant to receive. Instead of examining methods, the blame usually goes to the person who does not receive what they seek. We need to step back and look at this long and hard in today's church. God has provided us with a few different methods for deliverance. Even Jesus did not use the same methods with everyone He encountered. For example, His dialogue with the woman at the well in John 4 is akin to a counseling technique, while the woman with the issue of blood was delivered just by touching the hem of His garment as she was moved by her faith. The church is called to approach all matters of faith, healing, and deliverance in more than just a standard one-dimensional way.

This means counseling is a form of both healing and deliverance ministry and must be regarded as such. The purpose of counseling is to facilitate deliverance for those who need to be set free and facilitate healing for those who need healing. Counseling is needed when deliverance cannot come about through a two-or-three-minute process. It also is needed when a situation is deeper than what surface issue may exist on the surface. Counseling is needed when deliverance comes about over time.

Counseling at the altar...and off to the side

It is my belief that counseling should always be an option for those seeking healing and deliverance. This may seem impossible, especially given deliverance sessions at the altar are done as part of other services. In such settings, confidentiality and time become constraints. It would be out of order for a service to become all about counseling an individual, not to mention an ethics issue. This means ministers must address the issues of counseling when it comes up as part of a service or event in one of three ways.

- **Have trained and equipped counselors on staff, ready to take people aside with counseling issues:** It is advisable to have staff available for times such as this, for several reasons. The first is because not every issue can be solved on the altar, and sometimes what is stirred up by an altar call needs immediate attention. The second is because not every issue that arises can be handled quickly and quietly by one minister. As God gifts the Body of Christ for all issues, there is no reason to think only one minister can fix and heal all issues at hand. As we can see from prior chapters, the gifts God provides to the church as well as the five-fold ministry provide a complete balance. If someone is knowingly more qualified to handle something than the speaking or main minister, the person who is more qualified should be able to take someone off to the side and help them in greater detail. Counseling is a perfect example of this. The main speaker or facilitator should know those who counsel others, should be prepared for such a situation should it arise, and all involved should be duly trained and purposed for their tasks.

- **Offer counseling services for a later time, providing the information through a staff member or business card:** If the option to have someone else counsel an individual is unavailable, see to it that the individual receives information pertaining to counseling sessions, so they have the option to pursue counseling outside of the service at hand.

- **Offer a quiet and short word, encouraging the individual to speak to you or someone else after the event is over:** When giving words to people at the altar, put the microphone down or turn it off. If it becomes obvious that counseling is needed, quietly suggest to the individual that they speak to you after the service. Make counseling available during this time.

There will be occasions when all the above are needed, one of the above are needed, or a combination is needed. Having these options helps to maintain order and see that every need is met within the Body at all times.

The essential role of grace in counseling

The Word of God teaches that we are saved by grace through faith. Even though grace is often a common church word, it is not something well understood by modern believers. In many instances, grace is misapplied or misunderstood. Grace is not getting a good parking spot at the mall, nor is it an excuse to behave in any way desired at any time. Grace is the unmerited favor of God, something bestowed upon human beings as a testimony to the goodness of God and His saving nature.

Most of the time we discuss grace, it is discussed in the context of sin and God's forgiveness of our sins. The level we discuss grace on in this context is very elementary: it is the principle that God forgives our sins and saves us of no doing of our own, and that He offers us salvation even though He is under no obligation to do so. This is all true theologically, but there is a level of grace we don't often consider: that of healing and deliverance beyond the sense of salvation. There are many things that human beings encounter within their lifetimes that are beyond comprehension. Some people have seen and experienced things that wrench at the very concepts we have about life and challenge us in the ideals we often cling to as part of our belief systems. The struggles people have are often overwhelming and can cause even the person strongest in faith to question the who, what, where, when, and why of things. The way these realities shake us up are not intended to break our faith but show forth a deeper level of God's grace working within humanity. Deliverance proves that God is sovereign and that God can overcome evil with the utmost of goodness. It offers hope for the hurting, and a powerful light in the darkness. Counseling offers this form of deliverance as patients work through the process, one step at a time, and come to a place of victory that no one can take away from them. Through counseling, God reaches out His hand of redemption and heals some of the most unfathomable hurts, all by a means of His favor that none of us can rightly understand.

This makes the Christian counselor an agent of God's grace. Through the counseling process, the counselor walks in God's grace and also receives a greater sense and reassurance of the grace of God as each patient is brought to a purposed sense of hope, healing, and promise. The counselor's faith is reaffirmed, and the effectiveness of counseling is reassured, with each moment of grace that transforms one of God's people, all over again.

Examples of deliverance ministry worked through counseling

The examples of deliverance ministry are endless. The truth is that we could write books on each of the topics listed below, just in the proper protocol and procedure to bring about deliverance on these issues through counseling. Here we but scratch the surface and provide thinking and launching pads, as these issues are commonly seen through counseling. What I seek to examine here are the root causes of the issues listed below and ways a counselor can help someone at the root of these issues.

- **Church abuse:** One of the biggest scars marring the church today is the issue of church abuse. Stories abound of people who have been hurt, in one way or another, by a domineering leader, unkind so-called Christian believers, or actual physical or sexual abuses by people who are in the church. These situations create distrust not just for God, but for God's church system and for people within God's system. In the case of church abuse, the counselor must facilitate a sense of trust, because the root issue of this issue has been a violation of trust. This begins as trust is developed between the client and the counselor. A counselor is careful to represent the best of ministry, setting forth a sound foundation of trust by adhering to counselor's ethics and by seeing God work through the process. Emphasizing difference and pointing toward a sense of truth and a belief that Christians can be trusted helps to address this underlying issue which may be affecting someone hurt by church abuse.

- **Indoctrination/doctrine/cults:** Akin to church abuse are the issues of indoctrination, doctrine, and cults. These issues are difficult to address and require training when it comes to addressing the doctrinal issues and errors. When it comes to the heart of these issues, a person is dealing with deception and falling into deception. Deception is difficult to overcome and requires steady patience. When an individual realizes they have been deceived, they are forced to confront the reality they have run from under the guise of deception. Individuals who deal with deception go on to deal with other issues of trust, authority, order, and reality in their lives. A person dealing with deception needs help to deal with varied aspects of reality, including discernment, decision-making, and reorientation toward life. Cult living specifies every aspect of living, thus requiring an individual who is coming out of that situation to orient themselves once again to the everyday circumstances that come along in life.

- **Rape/sexual abuse:** Rape and sexual abuse are often two of the most traumatic human experiences. They are also far from uncommon. The level of violation someone experiences when they have been violated sexually is unspeakable. This work takes special training and patience, and a special anointing to bring forth love, grace, and healing in the midst of such a traumatic experience. A rape or sexual abuse survivor needs a special sense of grace and restoration within their lives. Sexual abuse and rape victims need time, hope, and healing as they come to terms with what happened to them, especially as details of the event unfold. Through the counseling process, sexual abuse victims and rape victims alike should be encouraged to express their feelings through discussion, emotion, and creative forms as a sense of empowerment, forgiveness, and moving forward comes forth from counseling. In instances of rape and/or sexual abuse, Christian counseling should double with mental health treatment, to ensure there are no gaps in care.

- **Abuse:** Above we spoke of sexual abuse. Here we will speak about abuse in general, and how counseling can help with any form of abuse. One of the mistakes people make in assessing abuse is to partition abuse by form. The truth is that abuse in any form is a violation of a person, and all forms of abuse or mistreatment can be damaging. Whether an individual has been physically, sexually, emotionally, spiritually, mentally, or economically abused, they need to come into a sense of healing and empowerment within their lives. All abuse victims need time, hope, and healing, as well as a sense of balance and restored confidence within themselves. Being abused is not an excuse to mistreat or abuse others, and this message must be conveyed through the healing process. Through the process, abuse survivors should pass from victimization to survivor and encouraged to express their feelings and process through discussion, emotion, and creative forms as a sense of empowerment, forgiveness, and moving forward comes forth from counseling.

- **Drug and alcohol abuse:** Drug and alcohol counseling have become a common fodder in the modern church. he one problem with modern drug and alcohol abuse counseling is that nobody quite agrees on how to handle this most sensitive issue within Christian circles. Counselors who pursue drug and alcohol abuse counseling must be trained for work in this area. If a Christian counselor is to be effective in drug and alcohol counseling, they must be prepared to be discerning, smart, alert, and non-enabling. This means the counselor cannot become a sub-par enabler, encouraging other members of the family and the user themselves to continue using via implied behaviors and means. A counselor cannot be fooled by the right words, right manipulations, and right mannerisms that enable a user to keep using. Drug and alcohol counseling is about reality: facing it, dealing with it, and helping users to face life one day at a time sober and empowered by the Holy Spirit. In cases of drug and alcohol abuse, a twelve-step program should be used along with Christian counseling.

Chapter Review

<u>Essay Questions</u>

Construct a well-written essay (minimum 5-8 sentences), answering the following question.

- Explain deliverance ministry in detail — what it is and its varied forms — and how Christian counseling is an effective and powerful deliverance ministry.

CHAPTER NINETEEN

Spiritual Warfare and Warfare Training in Counseling

He said, "Your name shall no longer be Jacob, but Israel;
for you have striven with God and with men and have prevailed."
- Genesis 32:28

Spiritual warfare is a common topic addressed in today's church. The context of spiritual warfare is often in a personal context, in the sense of an individual's specific and personal battles or attacks from the enemy. We do not often consider spiritual warfare in a bigger sense: that of true spiritual battle, where one's very life may be at stake in some way. Whether it is a physical battle, an emotional battle, a mental battle, or a spiritual battle, spiritual warfare is often a demonic operation to somehow take a person out. Spiritual warfare can also represent the trial one goes through when they are wrestling with God or others as they go through a growing process with God and their relationship with others may change. Spiritual warfare ministry often couples with deliverance, but the operation of spiritual warfare is far more intense, as the counselor engages in battle against the demonic realm in an attempt to help deliver the individual in question.

Spiritual warfare as an aspect of counseling is not for the faint of heart, nor is it an easy aspect of Christian counseling. It may be, by far, one of the most intense and difficult areas of Christian counseling. The required objectivity, balance, and non-emotional involvement must all come together, working in harmony, to help bring forth deliverance by spiritual power. It requires a counselor to know and recognize weaknesses and strengths within themselves, and also a keen spiritual sense to identify patterns, changes, shifts, and deceptions within a client. Counselors who operate in spiritual warfare must walk powerfully in both intercession and spiritual discernment.

In this chapter, we are going to look at both sides of spiritual warfare: that with an individual's struggle with God and others, and an individual's struggle with the demonic, and ways a Christian counselor can effectively operate through spiritual warfare within the counseling process.

Wrestling with God

In Genesis 32:28, we learn that Jacob wrestled with an angel of God, which represented God Himself. Jacob was victorious in battle with the angel of God, and the representation of this victory is signified in his name change. Jacob went from being "the deceiver" to Israel, which means "He who struggled with God and man and has overcome." This simple name change has often gone unstudied by many and overlooked in preaching. There is true significance, however, in this shift. Most people look at this passage in the Word as about no more than the struggle Jacob had with the angel. This assessment is incorrect on several levels, because we are missing the true spiritual meaning in the passage. The struggle Jacob had with the angel was symbolic of Jacob's wrestling with God. For his entire life, Jacob lived according to a certain standard of deception. He deceived his brother, he deceived his father, and he most likely deceived others in his life, because it was a pattern of operation. This pursuit of deception caused Jacob himself to be deceived – as he sowed, so he did reap – in his marriage to Leah and Rachel. Even in Genesis 32, found in prior verses, Jacob is still trying to work his magic as the deceiver – he attempts to work his manipulation on his brother, Esau, who he is to see after many years of separation. It is no accident, therefore, that the night before they are to meet, Jacob has this experience where he wrestles with God.

Jacob's encounter signifies a needed change within his life. Even though he lived a certain way throughout his entire life, Jacob was called to change. This change did not come about easily – Jacob wrestled with God over it. Why? Jacob knew how he operated, and even though he'd reaped what he'd sown through his marriages, Jacob's operation worked for him. It was familiar to him, comfortable, and a way of looking at the world and interacting with other people. Even though I am sure Jacob had lots of signs that this was not a good way to live, it was what he knew, and it was how he lived. Now, all of a sudden, God called him to change.

Jacob wrestled with God. Jacob wrestled with God because God called him to change. It was a struggle to transform into a new person, a new creature. Jacob knew what God was calling him to do, and he struggled with that change.

It is a mistake for us to assume the only way one wrestles with God is with an angel who comes down from the sky. The true wrestling with God is that which comes about as God calls us to change, and we struggle with that change. There are any number of ways we can "struggle with God." The most obvious way is our struggle with God to change. If God is calling us to change with others, it also means He is calling us to change in our relationship with Him. This change can be a change in behavior or interaction with humanity, as was the instance with Jacob. It can also be a change as God calls us into ministry, church leadership, a new call on our lives, or dealing with the concept of being chosen or set apart for a specific call or work. Whenever we go through a change in our relationship with God, we will go through a period of wrestling. We will battle our flesh and the Spirit as we walk out the call of God on our lives. Wrestling with God is not necessarily a bad thing; it is a human thing, something that comes as we die to the flesh and grow in the Spirit. Wrestling with God and winning doesn't mean God loses, it means that the flesh is defeated within us, and God brings us to victory in Him. As Jacob went through it, so too we go through it – and we wrestle through to the blessing, that we may wrestle with God…and win.

The Christian counselor is called to stand with the wrestler as they wrestle with God, helping and assisting in the process through listening, encouragement, guidance, and prayer. In this instance, the Christian counselor also serves as a mentor of sorts, helping the person as they come through their discoveries of God and self through this time.

Keeping the individual on track and focused during this time is the best work a counselor can do.

Wrestling with humans

The Word also clarifies that the name "Israel" did not just mean struggling and overcoming with God, but also struggling and overcoming with man, or humanity, as well. This overcoming is a dual meaning: to change, Jacob had to wrestle with both God and human beings. He, as the middle being in the equation, had to change his dealings with both. To obey God, he had to interact differently with others, as well. This is the wrestling with human beings: our adjustment to their change in how we interact with them. Whenever we go through a change as individuals, the change that comes forth can lead to conflict – and intense conflict, at that. People do not always understand these changes, nor do they always respond well to them. The wrestling we experience with others as we wrestle with God brings us to a place of power and realization in Christ. People may disbelieve an individual has changed (as those who heard of the Apostle Paul's conversion were still afraid of him for a time), or they may dislike the changes as a person's paradigm shifts away from the old and toward the new.

Wrestling with human beings can be just as difficult as wrestling with God, if not more so. The reason for this is simple: wrestling with others often means trying to figure out motives, assessments, thoughts, ideas, and beyond. It considers where a person comes from when attacked by another, and where the person is who is attacked and wrestling. Wrestling with humans is also complicated by the fact that a person may be wrestling more than one issue, role, concept, or person at one time. Even though we know that in a larger, spiritual sense we do not wrestle with people, but with the powers of darkness, the fact that people become conduits for these powers of darkness means shift, change, and complexity in relationship. Just because we are fighting opposing powers that are larger than we may see on the surface does not mean that we should allow people to mistreat us – and recognizing this in a larger sense is the key to victory when wrestling with others.

A Christian counselor has the unique position to encourage a person wrestling with others to remain true to God's course, even if this means leaving other people behind. The client should be encouraged to remain excited about God's work in their lives and remind them that there is always the purpose and possibility to meet new people better suited to the new place in which they are advancing. Wrestling with God and man means moving forward in a direction to which no one may understand, but with God, all know the relevance. The Christian counselor gets to bring the client back to the point of relevance. No matter the struggle with people, God brings us through the battle and back to a place in Him that is more centered, honest, and purposed than ever before.

Job and counseling

We don't hear much about the book of Job in the modern church, because the story of Job often doesn't fit with modern preaching. The church, therefore, is neglecting the important human process of wrestling. Instead of acknowledging the wrestle with God and man as part of human experience, people today are accused of being negative, brushed off with positive sayings, or encouraged to "confess" their circumstances away. We should never forget there is a fine line between speaking the things that be not as though they are and both denial and lying when that passage is taken out of context. A passage that pertains to prophecy is now used against people who are genuinely seeking God to grow to a new place in Him who may struggle in the process. This attitude is seen in our overall negativity toward Job: he is portrayed as being negative, complaining, having a bad attitude, having an issue with pride, and deserving to "go through" what he did, even though the Word does not endorse any such attitude. By making Job out to be a villain, the church fails to see its identity with him. Job wrestled with God and with man. He struggled to understand what happened to him, because what happened to him felt unjust. Looking at Job seriously reveals a man who did not just wrestle with God and man, he also overcame. Through his forty-year counseling session with God, Job came to a place where his struggle was understandable and purposed. The book of Job, therefore, is the meeting of struggle of God, man, and the ultimate ability to overcome.

Christian counselors need to pay special attention to the experience of Job to better serve their clients. There will be times during the wrestle that they may ask many questions, inquire to depths, and seemingly ask and seek on the same things over and over again. This does not mean a client is failing to learn — it means they are wrestling. The analogy of wrestling exists deliberately: because during a wrestling match, sometimes one person seems to be victorious, and at other times, it is another person. The match is not over until it is over and until a clear victory is at hand. The goal of every Christian counselor should match that of God's counsel position in the book of Job: to guide the individual through their process unto victory without enabling or babying. God provided the answers and the thought and also made Himself known through a comforting presence. Even though Job wrestled with man, God let Job know he was not alone. Christian counselors are privileged to do the same: let a wrestling person know they are not alone. Whether a person wrestles for four weeks or forty years, a Christian counselor is there with that person, serving God and man through the process.

Mental illness: the wrestling within

The level of spiritual warfare we have spoken of to this point has pertained to God and man — wrestling with where God calls us to be and wrestling with others as we pursue where God would have us to be. These different spiritual battles (which are often related) are those which are instigated from outside of an individual. They come about because God seeks to do something in us or someone else reacts to the work God is doing within us. We are now going to shift to a very specific aspect of spiritual warfare that is perhaps one of the most difficult areas to treat and confront: mental illness. I define mental illness as "the wrestling within" because it comes not from God, nor from others, but from a persistent way of viewing the world and others that is harmful to that individual. It is a wrestling within oneself, a captivity that is difficult to liberate.

A person who is deemed mentally ill displays certain thoughts, behavioral patterns, or actions that cause distress, either to the individual or others, that are deemed outside the normal realm of development within a culture's concept of socialization. These different mental disorders are grouped according to symptoms that seem to relate to the disorder, although in some cases, it is not always clear as to why or how. Despite many years of scientific study, there are no conclusive causes for mental illness. Research is still necessary to understand the role between mental illness and biochemical or biological causes. Some appear to have biological origin, but we don't understand enough about the connection to draw many conclusions. Regardless, mental illness often poses both biological and spiritual struggle.

Understanding mental illness to be a spiritual struggle does not mean we should approach mental attitude with an exorcist perspective. It does not mean those who struggle with varied forms of mental illness should be mistreated, abused, excluded from church, or treated as second-class because of their circumstances. Mental illness requires special training to handle, and a specific understanding of spiritual warfare to continually battle for the individual.

It's a mistake for a minister to tell a person who has been diagnosed with a mental disorder to stop taking their medications and ignore doctor's orders. Not only is doing so an open door to legal liability, it also opens the individual in question to spiritual invasion they may be unable to handle. What this means is a Christian counselor must all-the-more prepare for a spiritual battle when counseling a patient who is mentally ill, especially if they are believing God for healing or release of symptoms.

DSM-V

The DSM-V, known formally as *The Diagnostic and Statistical Manual of Mental Disorders, Fifth Edition*, is often nicknamed the "bible of mental disorders." It is so-called because it is the standard textbook by which mental disorders are categorized, defined, grouped, and evaluated. This book, published by the American Psychiatric Association, is used by mental health professionals to assess mental illness and assist in better ways to treat mental disorders of all sorts.

If a person has been diagnosed with a mental illness or disorder by a qualified and trained psychiatrist, psychotherapist, or other mental health professional, a person's behavioral or mental characteristics align with those to be classified as having a disorder.

The DSM-V continues to expand, and with that expansion comes an increasing number of diagnoses and issues that were not formerly classified as disorders or mental illnesses. I am in full agreement that psychiatry is going overboard in diagnosing and treating issues that are just a part of normal human existence. Every human being goes through different emotions facing loss, grief, or trauma. These experiences do not, in and of themselves, make an individual mentally ill. This fact, however, does not change the reality of those individuals who are mentally disordered or disturbed and need true care, warfare, and prayer as they go through various situations.

A Christian counselor should never diagnose or attempt to treat a mental illness without the proper training in psychiatry and psychotherapy. What is more, a Christian counselor should never attempt to undermine a diagnosis under the guise of faith healing or prayer. In the practice of ethics, Christian counselors should uphold dignity and never contradict prior diagnosis without concrete evidence to the contrary.

Medication

The most difficult area for Christian counselors is often in medication. Without a medical license, a counselor of any sort is forbidden from dispensing or prescribing medication to a client. I have found, however, that Christian counselors and ministers are seldom eager to prescribe medication – but to get clients to stop taking medications. The reason medication becomes an issue is over the debate of healing. If a person declares someone to be healed from a mental issue, the conclusion many come to is that the individual should stop taking their medications. There are many reasons why this is not advisable. The first is that it opens a Christian counselor and minister to liability. The second reason is that as medication often controls symptoms, recommending the cessation of medication can unleash uncontrollable behavior in the instance a person is not completely healed.

There is no question that many of the medications given to treat mental illnesses have their own side effects and are sometimes newly issued or poorly studied. Some are dangerous, powerful drugs that are questionable in their results. That having been said, when it comes to mental illness, the only way to treat some disorders at the current time is through medication. This means that with a person who is seriously mentally disordered, medication is the only way to combat the various thoughts, issues, and problems that may arise as part of their illness. By telling someone not to take their medications, a powerful aspect of their warfare is being removed from the equation, leaving them open to harm. When it comes to mental illness, medication can be an effective tool in battling the spiritual warfare that affects someone's life.

Warfare training in counseling

A Christian counselor trains themselves for spiritual warfare in counseling in five ways. These ways are education, specialization, training, preparation, and objectivity.

- **Education:** Do not undertake Christian counseling without proper education. It is important to know what your education allows you to do, and what you are trained to do by your education. Satan's best weapon is a person who thinks they are doing a good thing, or even a godly thing, but have no knowledge of what that really may be. We can pray all day but if we are not trained for what we are doing, misleading people will be inevitable. As a Christian counselor, the most powerful weapon you have for spiritual warfare is a good, comprehensive education.

- **Specialization:** I recommend all Christian counselors specialize in an area of Christian counseling. This does not mean that a Christian counselor cannot help someone with a different issue, but it does mean that most of the training and focus will go into developing Christian counseling as a ministry in a specified area. Most therapists and counselors specialize in certain areas of therapy, such as marriage and family therapy, domestic violence, drug and alcohol abuse, children, teens, abuse victims, etc. Specializing in a certain area gives the Christian counselor the ability to expansively study and research a specific area of counseling and develop strength in that area, versus approaching counseling by a hit-and-miss application. It also gives the Christian counselor the freedom to back away from something if they do not feel qualified to handle a situation.

- **Training:** Training does not begin and end with an educational degree. Training for counseling continues as a counselor researches new continuing education classes, seminars, developments, treatments, cases, and techniques to ever-expand their expertise in a specified area as a Christian counselor. It is essential a Christian counselor remains current in counseling practice as well as current on major issues, trends, and areas pertinent to Christian counseling and practice.

- **Preparation:** The Christian counselor must always be prepared. This means a check of the counselor's own spiritual walk from time to time through prayer, fasting, devotion to the Lord, purpose in the faith, and active in belief. A Christian counselor must be prepared for battle, both to defend their honor as a Christian counselor, and to defend the welfare of their client. A Christian counselor must be ready in season and out for the task of their work.

- **Objectivity:** We have already spoken of professional distance and emotional objectivity with clients. Here, in terms of spiritual warfare, it is essential the Christian counselor remain objective about themselves. A Christian counselor needs to know their own personal limits, boundaries, specialties, abilities, and have the foresight to operate in wisdom in all circumstances pertaining to clients. When a Christian counselor fails to hold themselves to a standard of objectivity, the enemy can manipulate circumstances and purposes away from healing and wholeness.

Chapter Review

<u>Short Answer</u>

Answer the following question in 1 to 3 sentences.

- How is mental illness "the wrestling within?" Why must Christian counselors be careful when warring spiritually for a mentally ill patient? How should a Christian counselor conduct themselves when dealing with someone who is mentally ill?

<u>Character Profiles</u>

Create an outline character sketch of the following figures in Bible counseling. Construct an outline on the life and work of the following individuals.

- Job
- Jacob

<u>Essay Questions</u>

Construct a well-written essay (minimum 5-8 sentences), answering the following question.

- Detail the experience of "wrestling with God and men" and how an individual can overcome through these processes by counseling.

CHAPTER TWENTY

Christian Counseling as Theory and Practice in Scenarios

What counsel you have given to one without wisdom!
What helpful insight you have abundantly provided!
- Job 26:3

Throughout this book, we have examined essential information and application to create success in Christian counseling. In this final chapter of the book, we are going to look at scenarios and apply Christian counseling assessment, technique, and recommendation. The scenarios presented in this chapter are hypothetical, but are based on real-life situations many Christians face in our modern times. This means the scenarios in this chapter relate to things going on within the church, in Christian relationships, and in Christians themselves.

Patient W and X – Male, 48 and Female, 47 (Married Couple)

- **Patient overview:** Patient W is a 48-year-old male and Patient X is a 47-year-old female. The two have been married for 29 years. They have three children, now all grown and out of the house. Patient W is a pastor and has been such for a little over a year. He has been a Christian since early in the marriage, which has been a source of contention between the couple and within the household. He discerned his call to ministry after many years of working unsuccessfully in several unfulfilling jobs. With the counsel of his apostle, he started to discern his call into the ministry. Patient X is a non-believer, with job experience opposite Patient W: Patient X has spent many years on a successful job and excelled in her work. The past year has caused an incomprehensible strain on the relationship.

From the very beginning, Patient W and Patient X have had a troubled marital relationship. Differences in beliefs, approaches in life, and different personalities have caused conflict. Patient W and Patient X do not enjoy one another as people, and do not respect one another. The three children of the marriage had difficult childhoods and teen years because of conflicts between Patient W and Patient X. One of their three children in particular, a girl, who is also the youngest child, married to escape the tensions at home and is now involved in an abusive relationship. Patient W claims to love his wife and believes she loves him, despite the fact that she has stated she does not for many years and does all in her power to push him away.

- **Patient W's Perspective:** Patient W admits to being a difficult spouse early in the relationship, including having an affair at a midway point in the relationship. He also admits to being difficult to live with but is hesitant to express what makes him feel he is difficult to live with. He believes that by staying with his wife all these years, he has worked to preserve his family and is proving he loves her. He blames the family's various financial struggles on his own inability to be successful in a career. At the same time, Patient W is frustrated and feels hurt and empty, because he feels he is unable to communicate the essence of his newly found Christian call with his unbelieving wife. He has spent many years angry that his wife does not show any interest in being a Christian and feels hurt that she cannot put aside her spiritual perspectives to support him in the pastorate.

- **Patient X's Perspective:** Patient X wants nothing to do with the entire counseling process; in fact, she did not want to attend counseling in the first place. She expresses no desire to remain in the marriage but does not say why she continues to stay. She does state that she will leave but does not say when. Her emphatic response is she is not ready to leave. She does not clarify what is holding her there. Patient X believes Patient W's new-found pastoral calling is just another attempt to make himself successful. She believes he will fail, and there is no reason for encouragement. It has drained already strained financial resources and she resents that this "pastor thing" is affecting her life. Patient X is likewise concerned her daughter will want to return home, also affecting her life. Patient X is clear that love is not keeping her in the relationship, but she does not clarify what is keeping her there. She does not love her husband, she resents her children, and now she resents her husband's pursuit of the pastorate.

- **Counselor's Perspective:** Based on what has been expressed by Patients W and X respectively, it is evident their marriage is in a grave state. What Patient W has expressed feeling from his wife, in terms of resentment, about wife is accurate. She is all the things he feels. She does not meet his needs. At the same time, he is incorrect in stating he believes she still loves him. This is an illusion Patient W has created to justify staying in the relationship. Patient W is attempting to apply a misguided sense of love to sustain a relationship that is already not sustainable by thinking if he loves her, he will continue to stay. Somewhere inside, he knows this, as is evident by the affair he had earlier in the relationship. On the other hand, he is not doing what he should be within the relationship, either. It is wonderful that Patient W has discovered a calling, but Patient W needs to step back and look at the dynamics involved in pursuing that calling. Patient W is pursuing a ministry call with an unsupportive partner. It is difficult enough to try and pursue a call, let alone attempting to pursue a call with someone who is totally unsupportive and apathetic at the same time. Patient W needs to look at himself, and why he feels like staying with his wife is enough of a statement of love to remain in the marriage. At the same time, he needs to respect her enough to realize the relationship is not going to change the way that it is.

Patient X has been clear in her speech and her intention, and there is no reason to disbelieve her statements. Yet she is still sending a mixed signal. Threatening divorce and failing to leave despite statements that she no longer loves her husband confuses Patient W, as he is assuming she stays out of love, just as he does. She needs to be clear in her reason for staying – is it due to money, convenience, vengeance, etc. She also needs to be honest enough to admit that while the pastorate is a source of contention for her, it is not the only source of contention.

- **Counselor's Advice:** Both Patient W and Patient X need to articulate their feelings, thoughts, and perspectives on their relationship. This is important because both parties have become so consumed by different aspects of the relationship, they have lost a sense of their individuality and personal responsibility in the relationship. Patient W's pastorate has become the subject matter within the relationship, and not the real issue. Behind that subject matter is Patient X's different beliefs when it comes to faith. While that is certainly a subject in their relationship, it is not the underlying issue.

Patient W and Patient X need to separate so each one can figure out what it is they are seeking and continue individual counseling in the meantime to regain a sense of identity with themselves and their purpose. In this position, both can determine what is best for them. It is not possible for them to figure this out together, because the relationship is not strong enough to weather out the storm. At this point in time, both need to discern things, with God's help, separately rather than together.

Patient Y – Female, 35 (Married female minister)

- **Patient overview:** Patient Y is a 35-year-old female. She is in her second marriage, which has, to date, lasted ten years. Her husband is secularly employed, although she wants him to serve as a pastor in one of her churches. While the marriage is relatively unassuming (not great but not terrible, either), the pressure to make him pastor is causing increased stress between them. She has a grown son and daughter, both from previous relationships. Her 21-year-old son is in the military and her 19-year-old daughter is in college. Patient Y is a Christian minister in the apostolic office and has been in ministry for approximately eight years. It has been a difficult eight years of ministry. She has watched the different phases of ministry and the different trends of leaders through her time in ministry. When people told her to pastor, she served as a pastor. When she thought evangelism was the key, she worked as an evangelist. For the past five years, Patient Y has gone in and out of the dynamics of pastoring, going through different phases to try and make the church work. Now Patient Y has reached a point where she is tired of trying so hard to make her ministry work. She has struggled without adequate help, leadership, and membership for the entire duration. It is her desire to be successful, but the successes that interest her are in a commercial sense. She seeks a high-paying salary and thinks ministry is about what happens on television. Patient Y desires the ambitions of fame and fortune, and resents the fact that her husband, family, and church members do not feel the same way about ministry as she does.

- **Patient Y's Perspective:** Patient Y wants more from life than she currently is experiencing. She wants more from her ministry. She wants to be able to operate in ministry in the way she thinks ministry should go. It is frustrating to her that she has spent so many years in ministry and finds everyone so uncooperative. She admits to going through periods where she wants to walk away from ministry. Patient Y wants to figure out how to get to a better place. She is seeking counseling for direction on how to make her ministry better.

- **Counselor's Perspective:** Patient Y has an inflated perspective of herself and her work, without doing the proper leadership. She is not being a leader to her people and not fully assuming her leadership role. She is not doing the work of an apostle. Patient Y needs to seriously examine her call and assess whether she is called to the office she seeks to pursue. Ministry is about a lot more than being on television and it is wrong for her to bully people in her life into accepting positions to try and make her life easier. She needs to step back and examine herself.

- **Counselor's Advice:** Patient Y needs solid ministerial leadership in the form of an apostolic covering. She needs to pursue self-examination and truly discern, with the help of her leader, the office she believes she is called to. Patient Y needs to learn how to become a leader. This will come about with a strong Scriptural understanding of the apostle and of leadership. If in resolving some of these issues she still finds such intense dissatisfaction in ministry, she needs to look at what she is attempting to gain in her life through ministry.

Patient Z – Male, 20 (single college-age male)

- **Patient overview:** Patient Z is a 20-year-old male. He is single and a student at a Christian college. While he likes college, he is not finding his current major to be of interest to him, which is physics. He is, however, looking to see through his education to the end. Patient Z is wrestling with feelings of same sex attraction in his life. He's not exactly sure where he fits on the spectrum, but he feels guilty about any feelings he may have. He feels dirty and unlovable by God. He also worries he will never find anyone who truly loves him in his life. He is afraid to tell his family about his struggles, because he believes they will disown him.

- **Patient Z's Perspective:** Patient Z feels confused and guilty. He was identified from the time he first realized his same sex attraction by that attraction. Now he is unsure of who he is, where he is going, and what he should do. He feels lost and rejected by his friends and family, and unable to share what he is going through with them. As his family is staunchly Christian, he believes rejection will follow if he ever reveals his issues.

- **Counselor's Perspective:** Patient Z has not developed himself as a person. As a teen, he came to identify himself by a sexual identity. This means in assuming this was who he was, Patient Z did not expand himself in other ways. Now that he is seeking to forsake that identity, he is in a state of disequilibrium, because he does not understand himself fully. Who he thought he was, now he questions. Patient Z is in a state to seek balance, and it is very wise he is seeking help and advice from a third-party counselor.

- **Counselor's Advice:** Patient Z needs to take some time and discover himself in every sense: both in sexual identity and as a person in general. Self-discovery is a lifelong process that does not begin nor end with one's sexual attractions, nor does it mean he should forsake his sexual identity. He needs to take some time and develop himself as a person through interests, pursuits, beliefs, and discovering his calling from God. It is also important that Patient Z begins to figure out some things in life for himself, separate from his family's influence. This is not because his family's influence is bad, but simply because he is becoming an adult and there will most likely be many choices and decisions he will face, and his family may approve or disapprove of any number of them. He needs to pursue godly friendships and relationships that will help him come to a place of understanding about who he is as a child of God, supporting and accepting him as he is, without contradiction of any part of himself, and empowered in that identity. It is recommended he continues counseling as he pursues this journey.

Patient A – Male, 8 (Male child)

- **Patient overview:** Patient A is an 8-year-old male. He has been having some behavioral issues at school. The school district recommended he see a doctor, who has diagnosed him with an autism spectrum disorder. He is largely non-verbal and has a tendency toward violent outbursts. His mother, a recently divorced 39-year-old woman, is a single parent to Patient A and his sister, a twelve-year old girl. Patient A's mother has brought him for Christian counseling assessment, in the hopes that Christian counseling can assist him in some of his behaviors.

- **Patient A's Perspective:** Patient A speaks little but likes to play and especially to color. His drawings are full of big swirls and bright colors. He likes to do what he likes to do.

- **Counselor's Perspective:** Patient A's issues are complicated. It is obvious that the school Patient A is attending is unable to meet the special and unique circumstances he has. It's also obvious that Patient A's mother is not receiving the right help, assistance, and advice to help Patient A.

- **Counselor's Advice:** Patient A needs to receive proper therapeutic care from a qualified mental health professional. Autism spectrum matters are beyond the bounds of Christian counseling, although there's nothing to be said that a Christian counselor can't supply advice or supplement help if qualified to do so. Recommendations include placing Patient A in a school or school program that can help accommodate his special learning needs. Patient A's mother also needs to explore counseling for herself, to help her understand her child's special needs and outlet the thoughts and feelings she is having as a result of her divorce and single parenthood.

Patient B – Female, 15 (female teenager)

- **Patient overview:** Patient B is a 15-year-old female. She has come to counseling at the force of her parents, who have noticed she is acting strangely. They are unhappy with her grades at school and have noticed a change in her attire. She is wearing all-black and dressing as a "Goth." Out of frustration, they have sent her to counseling because they want the behavior to stop. As Christians, they are embarrassed by her attire and what people in their circles are saying about them as parents.

- **Patient B's Perspective:** Patient B doesn't get what the big deal is. She is not sure if she wants to be a Christian anymore because of her parent's behavior toward her. She has been repeatedly grounded, they took away her cell phone and are on her all the time about her grades and her friends. If that's what it means to be a Christian, who wants to be one? Her biggest interests are gothic poetry, such as Edgar Allen Poe, music, and writing herself. She doesn't feel she needs counseling, she thinks she needs to get away from her parents.

- **Counselor's Perspective:** Patient B is going through teenage exploration that is being perceived as a rebellion by her parents. As her parents respond negatively to her, she responds back, with even more outrageous behavior. They are also making assumptions about her based on how she is dressing and acting. Not only are her parents not being a Christian witness to her, but they are also driving her deeper into her state of being.

Patient B is in a state of self-exploration, where she is trying to decide how she perceives the world. This is another phase in that development, and she may or may not at some point "grow out of it." Making such a huge fuss over her interest in such things is not going to make them go away. This is also a good lesson for her in understanding that, whether right or wrong, others do judge people based on outward appearance. As she is approaching adulthood, Patient B needs to understand the power of choice, and that we cannot make good choices to defy or rebel against others. This pertains to being a Christian but also pertains to life in general.

- **Counselor's Advice:** Patient B's parents should attend counseling to learn better techniques to communicate with their daughter, because their interactions have, up to this point, been extremely unproductive. The bottom-line issue is a severe communication disconnect and misunderstanding between the two. Patient B also should continue to attend counseling. She needs to develop trust and rapport with an individual outside of her household, to see that not all authority interacts with her in the same way. Patient B needs encouragement to learn alternative ways of self-expression: developing her writing, her interest in music, etc. rather than seeing the only way to express herself as an external experience. Patient B should also find a youth-based ministry group to help her see Christianity and the Christian experience as something relatable to her, and applicable to her life, so she can make a choice about it based on her own experience, rather than relying on that of her parents to make the choice for her.

Patient C – Male, 60 (Widowed male)

- **Patient overview:** Patient C is a 60-year-old widowed male. He lost his wife due to complications from HIV approximately two years ago. He discovered her HIV diagnosis because of an affair she had with a male acquaintance of theirs, one year prior to her death. Her HIV progression was rapid, from diagnosis to death, most likely because she had been infected for several years before diagnosed. It turned out this was not her first affair and explained a sexual distance between them that occurred over a course of about twenty years. Although Patient C has been tested for HIV and tested negative, his wife's diagnosis and death haunt him. For many years he acted as her caregiver, believing she was ill with cancer. He is hurt and wounded, and as he retired five years earlier to care for her, he is now left with the haunts of memories, lies, and offenses. His four adult children, ages 41, 39, 36 and 33, are embittered toward their father, after discovering what happened to their mother. Feeling disconnected from his family, he does not know where to turn. At his age, he is uncertain of what is next for him. He is angry at God for allowing his wife to get sick and die. As a nominal churchgoer for several years, his experiences over the past few years make him want to experience God in a new way, to help with his loneliness.

- **Patient C's Perspective:** Patient C is embittered toward his late wife. He feels he gave her everything he could, only to experience intense rejection from her. He has grown over time to hate her, and to hate God for what has happened to her and to him. As he continues to age, he wants to reconcile himself to God. He also hopes that, as he works out his issues, he can somehow reconcile with his children.

- **Counselor's Perspective:** Patient C has a difficult journey of healing ahead of him. In his process to reconcile with God, he must also reconcile himself with the relationship he had with his wife.

- **Counselor's Advice:** Patient C needs a guided approach to his healing process. It will work progressively, through the depth of forgiveness that must transform his life. By opening Patient C up to new experiences and identifying gifts and outlets for him in his life, Patient C can walk the powerful road of healing and forgiveness. At a later point in time, Patient C should consider counseling with his children, as well as encouraging each one of them to seek it out as individuals.

Chapter Review

Essay Questions

Given the information below, create a Counselor Perspective and Advice on the following patient scenarios.

- Patient O is a 45-year-old woman who is newly divorced. Her divorce came because of her memories of sexual abuse in childhood, which recently came back to her in flashes. Her husband was unsympathetic to her experiences and unkind and began having an affair with a much younger woman. Dealing with her recent divorce and flashbacks of abuse has been very traumatic for her. To make matters worse, she recently discovered the woman her husband is now living with (the woman who he had the affair with) is pregnant, when Patient O had been unable to conceive all through her marriage to her ex-husband. Patient O feels blighted, cursed, and unloved.

- Patients P and Q are a 32- and 35-year-old man and woman. They have a reasonably good marriage but want to discover tools to help strengthen their marriage even more. Their 3-year-old and 5-year-old boys are a handful and make time together difficult. They do not want to have problems later, so are seeking ways to develop tools and tips to prevent issues down the line.

- Patient R is a 16-year-old boy. His parents are devout Christians, but he is ambiguous about faith. His parents have sent him to counseling because they are concerned about the influence of his friends, who are into heavy drinking. One of his friends also recently overdosed on drugs and committed suicide. His parents don't know he has been sleeping with his girlfriend, who recently got pregnant. They secretly terminated the pregnancy without parental knowledge, and his parents have not found out. With so many things going on in his life and so many varied concerns,

Patient R is mildly uncommunicative, but willing to talk when reasoned with on his level.

- Patient S is a 25-year-old woman who was diagnosed with schizophrenia as a teenager. She goes through periods where she does not take her medication, and frequently claims to hear voices, those of which she believes are angels talking to her. She dislikes her medications because it makes her feel as if she has no feet and she dislikes the stability it brings. Patient S's pursuit of counseling is to receive healing so she no longer has to take her medication; however, it is difficult to get her to commit to disciplines and to show up regularly.

- Patient T is a 30-year-old man who is discerning a call from God to serve as an evangelist but is running into opposition. His family disapproves of his calling and his fiancée has threatened to call off the wedding if he persists in this "crazy ministry thing." He is unsure of what to do and how to convince his family that his call is from God.

CONCLUSION

Christian Counseling as a New Theory and Practice

This I recall to my mind,
Therefore I have hope.
- Lamentations 3:21

G od does not promise humanity an easy existence. We know of the promise of the new heavens and new earth to come (Isaiah 65:17, Isaiah 66:22, 2 Peter 3:13), but in the meantime, humanity struggles. Humanity struggles with the ravages of sin, sickness, confusion, despair, and evil. At the same time, humanity has the great power and ability to overcome all of these negatives, through healing, deliverance, and forgiveness. In this modern world, it seems like the hurts of humanity are endless. It seems like every time we watch television, turn on the internet, read a newspaper, or hear the news, we are hearing about greater disparages of the human condition. The more humanity wrestles and the more the church wrestles, the more relevant Christian counseling continues to become. It is relevant enough for us to have examined this book, and call both the church's leaders and counselors to offer its counsel to the church, to grow in purpose, once again, to re-establish relevance. God is healing us through counseling, but it is a new understanding of counseling and counsel: we, here, stand on the verge of Christian counseling as a new theory and practice.

I have spent several years working in counseling and therapy, both as a receiver of therapy and as a Christian counselor and ministerial therapist. I know from these personal experiences that my own healing and therapy didn't even begin until I became serious in my relationship with God, and know the same is true for those who too seek healing and therapy today. Through these processes, I have seen many who have been saved, healed, and delivered, and at the same time, I have seen many who never made that leap to fully trust in God and receive their healing. Despite the many success stories, we often find ourselves, as counselors and therapists, wondering what we have done wrong to lose the few that do not seem to benefit no matter what measures are taken toward their healing. Too often Christian counselors believe therapy begins and ends in a healing line, with the race to find the "right" minister to lay hands on the patient, to begin and end their healing process all in one motion. Some believe everything about Christian life is a matter of self-will and simply insist upon the emphasis to transform an individual within themselves. Then we have the extreme of secular counseling, which tends to diminish patient responsibility for personal actions, blames everything on biochemical imbalance to prescribe medication which covers symptoms, and does not process a patient toward effective healing of soul, mind, spirit, and body. With both sides staunchly believing themselves to be right, wherein does the answer lie?

This question is one both conventional and Christian counselors and therapists must stop and think about. For many years, counseling has been divided by those who use secular methods and those who use Christian methods. Neither side in this debate seems willing to budge, considering that perhaps the other side has something to contribute. Both insist they are right to the detriment of their patients. They overlook the gaps of patients who walk away, unsuccessful in process and without answers as to why the success rate hovers, not increasing.

Both Christian counseling and secular counseling have about the same success and failure rate. The reason for this is because they both need one another, but do not acknowledge it. Secular counseling can fill in gaps within Christian counseling, as Christian counseling can help fill the gaps of secular counseling. Both are part of the same process toward healing. With the truth about effective counseling lying somewhere in between the two, it only makes logical sense that combining the best of both makes for powerful change, transformation, and healing in the lives of patients.

The merging of both can only meet powerfully through Christian counseling. By applying the fundamentals presented in this book, we find effective methods to bridge the gap between both Christian and secular counseling, transforming the process into one where counselors of any sort become effective healers and patients become effectively healed. Acknowledging that healing is a process which counselors can participate in as agents of God's grace, this book is more than just a transformation of Christian or secular counseling we are creating a new theory and practice for understanding the foundations of Christian counseling. In transforming the very concept of Christian counseling, and centering it on healing, we find the perfect balance to facilitate a God-centered, whole-being approach to therapy and healing for patients.

In this realization, each individual counselor, minister, and therapist is called to examine their methods in counseling, whatever they may be and whatever their source. We are being called to accountability; to finally step up and, instead of following common courses of action and common mentality, be responsible for the methods, actions, and intents that we rest on as people involved in the healing process. Too often therapists and counselors pass responsibility on to their patients when methods do not seem to work. While sometimes it is the case that a patient is not ready for the next steps in his/her healing process, sometimes it is a sign that the therapeutic method is broken, and in need of fixing. We can see from our extensive look at Christian counseling that much of counseling's practice is broken and in need of mature, responsible therapists to practice a healed and whole theory for counseling practice and application.

I said earlier in this book that counseling is a markedly different method of revelation than preaching or teaching. For this reason, preachers and ministers often have difficulty in therapeutic approach. In preaching, we handle revelation by a "drive-by" sort of approach. God gives the preacher a revelation and they give it to everyone, and hope everyone will receive and apply it. In counseling, the revelation is received by the patient, and the counselor, minister, or therapist simply assists in their discovery of that revelation. Counselors are treasure-hunters, bringing forth the incredible gold from earthen vessels, drawing out revelation, understanding, and knowledge as we use the methods set forth in this book to bring about the whole person, the best God has for everyone to be. If we rightly study the methods laid out here and remain open to the revelation which we receive as therapists, ministers, and counselors, it will be of greater benefit to those we assist and help in their healing process. To those who are hurting and in need of help, we likewise can be of greater support and blessing because we not only understand what God is revealing to us, but what He is revealing to them as well.

Let us not forget that within these pages, we are called to stand as healers rather than clinicians, and prophetic voices rather than diagnosticians. The human element is sadly missing from conventional practice, and we cannot ever underestimate the power of empowering the broken, wounded soul as people gifted by God to deliver a message of hope and healing to humanity. That is the essence of our new theory and practice for therapist, counselor, minister, and patient: to experience hope and healing in a dying and hurting world. Christians are called to be agents of change, being radically challenging voices in situations whereas silence would ordinarily prevail as the old paradigm rests securely in its comfort zone of control. Here we stand, in these days before Jesus returns, as John the Baptist did. We are called to herald this new shift toward the things of God, the ways of God, and the methods of God, and remind people that the day is now to repent, change ways, turn around, and become healed and whole; for the Kingdom of Heaven is at hand (Matthew 3:1).

REFERENCES

Introduction

[1]"Counseling." Merriam-Webster Online Dictionary. http://www.merriam-webster.com/dictionary/counseling. Accessed November 12, 2012.

Chapter 2

[1]"Psychoanalysis." http://en.wikipedia.org/wiki/Psychoanalysis. Accessed on November 18, 2012.

- "Id, Ego And Super-Ego." http://en.wikipedia.org/wiki/Id,_ego,_and_super-ego Accessed on November 18, 2012.
- "Psyche." http://en.wikipedia.org/wiki/Psyche_%28psychology%29. Accessed on November 18, 2012.
- "Psychoanalysis." http://en.wikipedia.org/wiki/Psychoanalysis. Accessed on November 18, 2012.
- "Psychosexual Development." http://en.wikipedia.org/wiki/Psychosexual_development. Accessed on November 18, 2012.
- "Sigmund Freud." http://en.wikipedia.org/wiki/Sigmund_Freud. Accessed on November 18, 2012.
- "Sublimation." http://en.wikipedia.org/wiki/Sublimation_%28psychology%29. Accessed on November 18, 2012.

Chapter 3

- "Analytical Psychology." http://en.wikipedia.org/wiki/Analytical_psychology. Accessed on November 19, 2012.
- "Carl Jung." http://en.wikipedia.org/wiki/Carl_Jung. Accessed on November 19, 2012.
- "Collective Unconscious." http://en.wikipedia.org/wiki/Collective_unconscious
- "Complex (Psychology)." http://en.wikipedia.org/wiki/Complex_%28psychology%29. Accessed on November 19, 2012.
- "Extraversion And Introversion." http://en.wikipedia.org/wiki/Extraversion_and_introversion#Introversion . Accessed on November 19, 2012.
- "Myers-Briggs Type Indicator." http://en.wikipedia.org/wiki/Myers-Briggs_Type_Indicator#Type_dynamics_and_development. Accessed on November 19, 2012.
- "Jungian Archetypes." http://en.wikipedia.org/wiki/Jungian_archetypes. Accessed on November 19, 2012.
- "Personality Psychology." http://en.wikipedia.org/wiki/Personality_psychology
- "Synchronicity." http://en.wikipedia.org/wiki/Synchronicity. Accessed on November 19, 2012.

Chapter 4

[1]"Individual Psychology." http://en.wikipedia.org/wiki/Individual_psychology. Accessed on November 16, 2012.
[2] Ibid.
[3]Ibid.
[4]Ibid.
[5]"Alfred Adler." http://en.wikipedia.org/wiki/Alfred_Adler. "Alfred Adler." http://en.wikipedia.org/wiki/Alfred_Adler

- "Alfred Adler." http://en.wikipedia.org/wiki/Alfred_Adler. Accessed on November 16, 2012.
- "Inferiority Complex." http://en.wikipedia.org/wiki/Inferiority_complex. Accessed on November 16, 2012.
- "Psychodynamics." http://en.wikipedia.org/wiki/Psychodynamic. Accessed

on November 16, 2012.
- "Teleology." http://en.wikipedia.org/wiki/Teleology. Accessed on November 16, 2012.

Chapter 5

[1]"Abraham Maslow." http://en.wikipedia.org/wiki/Abraham_Maslow. Accessed on November 17, 2012.
[2] Ibid.
[3] Ibid.

- "Abraham Maslow." http://en.wikipedia.org/wiki/Abraham_Maslow. Accessed on November 17, 2012.
- "Humanistic Psychology." http://en.wikipedia.org/wiki/Humanistic_psychologist. http://en.wikipedia.org/wiki/Abraham_Maslow. Accessed on November 17, 2012.
"Self-actualization." http://en.wikipedia.org/wiki/Self-actualization. http://en.wikipedia.org/wiki/Abraham_Maslow. Accessed on November 17, 2012.

Chapter 6

[1]"Karen Horney." http://en.wikipedia.org/wiki/Karen_Horney. Accessed on November 17, 2012.

- "Karen Horney." http://en.wikipedia.org/wiki/Karen_Horney. Accessed on November 17, 2012.
- Neo-Freudianism." http://en.wikipedia.org/wiki/Neo-Freudian. Accessed on November 17, 2012.

Chapter 7

- "Controversial Discussions." http://en.wikipedia.org/wiki/Controversial_discussions. Accessed on November 20, 2012.
- "Melanie Klein." http://en.wikipedia.org/wiki/Melanie_Klein. Accessed on November 20, 2012.
- "Play Therapy." http://en.wikipedia.org/wiki/Play_therapy. Accessed on November 20, 2012.

Chapter 8

[1]"Erich Fromm." http://en.wikipedia.org/wiki/Erich_Fromm. Accessed on November 23, 2012.

- "Biophilia Hypothesis." http://en.wikipedia.org/wiki/Biophilia_hypothesis. Accessed on November 23, 2012.
- "Erich Fromm." http://en.wikipedia.org/wiki/Erich_Fromm. Accessed on November 23, 2012.

Chapter 9

[1]"B.F. Skinner." http://en.wikipedia.org/wiki/B._F._Skinner. Accessed on November 22, 2014.
[2]Ibid.

- "Behaviorism." http://en.wikipedia.org/wiki/Behaviorism
- "B.F. Skinner." http://en.wikipedia.org/wiki/B._F._Skinner

Chapter 10

- "Christian Counseling." http://en.wikipedia.org/wiki/Christian_counseling. Accessed on November 25, 2012.

ABOUT THE AUTHOR

Dr. Lee Ann B. Marino, Ph.D., D.Min., D.D.

Dr. Lee Ann B. Marino, Ph.D., D.Min., D.D. (she/her) is "everyone's favorite theologian" leading Gen X, Millennials, and Gen Z with expertise in leadership training, queer and feminist theology, general religion, and apostolic theology. She has served in ministry since 1998 and was ordained as a pastor in 2002 and an apostle in 2010. She founded what is now Sanctuary Apostolic Fellowship Empowerment (SAFE) Ministries in 2004. Under her ministry heading Dr. Marino is founder and Overseer of Sanctuary International Fellowship Tabernacle (SIFT) (the original home of National Coming Out Sunday) and The Sanctuary Network, and Chancellor of Apostolic Covenant Theological Seminary (ACTS).

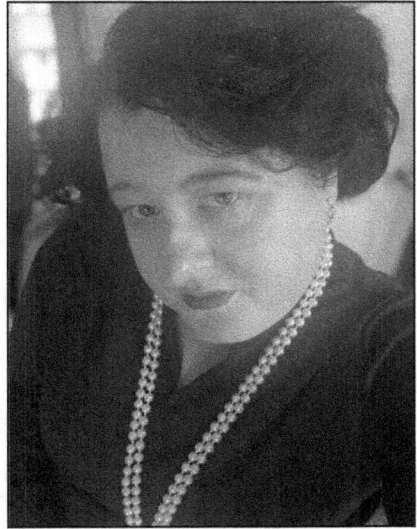

Affectionately nicknamed "the Spitfire," Dr. Marino has spent over two decades as an "apostle, preacher, and teacher" (2 Timothy 1:11), exercising her personal mandate to become "all things to all people" (1 Corinthians 9:22). Her embrace of spiritual issues (both technical and intimate) has found its home among both seekers and believers, those who desire spiritual answers to today's issues.

Dr. Marino has preached throughout the United States, Puerto Rico, and Europe in hundreds of religious services and experiences throughout the years. A history maker in her own right, she has spent over two decades in advocacy, education, and work for and within minority spiritual communities (including African American, Hispanic, and LGBTQ+). She has also served as the first woman on all-male synods, councils, and panels, as well as the first preacher or speaker welcomed of a different race, sexual orientation, or identity among diverse communities. Today, Dr. Marino's work extends to over 150 countries as she hosts the popular *Kingdom Now* podcast, which is in the top 20 percentile of all podcasts worldwide. She is also the author of over 35 books and the popular Patheos column, *Leadership on Fire*. To date, she has had five bestselling titles within their subject matter: *Understanding Demonology, Spiritual Warfare, Healing, and Deliverance: A Manual for the Christian Minister*; *Ministry School Boot Camp: Training for Helps Ministries, Appointments, and Beyond*; *Discovering Intimacy: A Journey Through the Song of Solomon*; *Fruit of the Vine: Study and Commentary on the Fruit of the Spirit*; and *Ministering to LGBTQ+ (and Those Who Love Them): A Primer for Queer Theology* (and its accompanying workbook).

As a public icon and social media influencer, Dr. Marino advocates healthy body image (curvy/full-figured), representation as a demisexual/aromantic, and albinism awareness as a model. Known to those she works with, she is a spiritual mom, teacher, leader, professor, confidant, and friend. She continues to transform, receiving new teaching, revelation, and insight in this thing we call "ministry." Through years of spiritual growth and maturity, Dr. Marino stands as herself, here to present what God has given to her for any who have an ear to hear.

For more information, visit her website at kingdompowernow.org.

www.ingramcontent.com/pod-product-compliance
Lightning Source LLC
Chambersburg PA
CBHW081407270326
41931CB00016B/3400